CW00487351

THE HAMMER AND THE ANVIL ⊘ LARISSA REISNER

The Hammer and the Anvil

Dispatches from the Frontline of the Russian Civil War 1918-1919

Larissa Reisner

Translated by Jack Robertson
Introduction by Judy Cox

a Redwords book

REDWORDS

The Hammer and the Anvil: Dispatches from the Frontline of the Russian Civil War 1918-1919
By Larissa Reisner,
A new translation by Jack Robertson

First published by Redwords, March 2021

Set in 11/14 Ehrhardt MT
Design and production Roger Huddle
Printed by Halstan Press, Amersham HP6 6HJ

Paperback: 978-1-912926-91-6
Kindle: 978-1-912926-92-3
e-pub: 978-1-912926-93-0

Redwords is linked to Bookmarks: the socialist bookshop
1 Bloomsbury Street, London WC1B 3QE

bookmarksbookshop.co.uk

✪ CONTENTS

✪ ACKNOWLEDGEMENTS Jack Robertson

The idea of translating and publishing a more comprehensive
selection of Larissa Reisner's frontline dispatches from the
Russian Civil War, in English, was first mooted at a meeting held
in Tony Cliff and Chanie Rosenberg's front room in Hackney,
in the late 1990s. At that time, the British Museum Library
held copies of Reisner's collected works, in Russian, in two
volumes, dated 1928. The second volume comprised eye-witness
accounts of the revolutionary events which took place in Weimar
Germany in 1923 and 1924. Extracts from these reports were
translated by Richard Chappell and published by Pluto Press in
1977, with the title *Hamburg at the Barricades*.
The first volume includes her earlier dispatches from the years
1918 and 1919 when she filed regular reports from the frontline
of the Russian Civil War. These were first published as regular
reports in *Izvestia*, the bulletin of the newly-formed Petrograd
Soviet. A decade later, they appeared in a Russian language
compilation, entitled *The Front*, or *Frontline (Фронт)*. The
translations in this book are from this period and concentrate

on the crucial events which took place in and around the naval base at Kazan. Control of this strategic intersection on the River Volga was vital because of its proximity to Moscow and its position on the main arterial through-route to the Russian capital, via Nizhny Novgorod. What happened in Kazan would determine either the downfall or the survival of the October Revolution. Fragments from these writings began to appear in English translations towards the end of the 1940s and some extracts punctuate Cathy Porter's biography, *Larissa Reisner*, published by Virago in 1988.

Work on the unabridged translations which feature in this book – apart from the chapter from Trotsky's autobiography – were long delayed but eventually started at the beginning of the coronavirus outbreak in 2020. Special thanks are due to those individuals who assisted during the subsequent months, mainly by remote. Foremost among these are: George Boulton, for taking the time to read and comment upon the fidelity of the finished translations to the Russian original; Katie Griffin and Katie McElvanney for their remarks and observations on specific chapters; and Jeremy Hicks of the Russian Department at Queen Mary & Westfield College for his unstinting help and advice. | Thanks are also due to the proof-reader Carol Williams, to Colm Bryce and Dave Gilchrist at Bookmarks and to the design wizard Roger Huddle, at Redwords.

Extraordinary documentary footage of the events described by Larissa Reisner in these chapters can now be seen in the final 30 minutes of Dziga Vertov's pioneering 1919 film, *Anniversary of the Revolution* (in the section entitled *The Czechoslovak Front*), which has recently been restored to its former glory by the Russian cine-archivist, Nikolai Izvolov, and is now available online.

December 2020

✪ INTRODUCTION Judy Cox

Larissa Reisner embodied the dynamic and creative spirit of Russia's revolutionary years: she was a poet and journalist, a revolutionary and a soldier. She took part in not one but two great revolutionary moments – the Russian Revolution of 1917-18 and the German Revolution of 1923. In this edition, Jack Robertson has undertaken the task of translating some of her most important articles into English from the original source. For that, we owe him a debt of gratitude.

Larissa Reisner was born in 1895 in Russian-occupied Poland into a family who held increasingly progressive views. Larissa's father was a Professor of Law who came to embrace socialism and corresponded with Vladimir Lenin. The Tsarist dictatorship did not tolerate any dissent and in 1903, Larissa and her family were forced to move to Berlin. In the German capital, the Reisners emersed themselves in socialist politics. Larissa later recalled meeting luminaries of the German Social Democratic Party, including August Bebel and Karl Liebknecht.

In 1905, peaceful protesters marching through the Russian capital St Petersburg were fired on by troops in what became known as Bloody Sunday. The massacre sparked a revolution which swept across Russia and its empire. In the aftermath of this revolt, the Reisner family moved back to St Petersburg, where Larissa graduated from school and, with her family's support, enrolled at the University of St Petersburg, which reluctantly accepted a handful of women students. Larissa had begun writing when she was still at school and in the pre-war years she established a growing reputation in St Petersburg's literary circles.

Larissa was twenty when the First World War broke out in August 1914. The poets she had looked up to became apologists for imperialist slaughter, like many leading figures in the international socialist movement. Larissa and her family not only opposed the war, they desperately sought ways to organise active opposition. They pawned their possessions to fund an anti-war publication, *Rudin*, which satirised those erstwhile socialists who collapsed into support for Russian chauvinism and war-mongering. The journal collapsed when the Reisner's funds ran out.

In 1916, Larissa took a steamer trip on the Volga with university friends. Her letters reveal her acute sense of the political unrest that was fermenting in the country. She wrote to her parents:

And another thing: we needn't fear for Russia. In the little sentry-boxes and market villages – along all the moorings of this vast river everything is irrevocably decided here, they know – everything, forgive nobody and forget nothing. And when the time comes, they will pass sentence and exact punishments such as have never before been seen. I am sometimes exhausted by helpless presentiments; if only the string doesn't snap too soon, if only these calm and terrible deeds don't remain mere words. But it's everywhere, beyond the yellowing forest edges, beyond the islands and rapids. And the elements are never mistaken.

In February 1917, the string snapped. On International Women's Day the anger of the women queuing for food coalesced with the grievances of women in the factories and exploded onto the streets of St Petersburg. The women ignited the February Revolution and unleashed a huge social movement. Within a few weeks, the Tsar had been forced to abdicate in favour of the Provisional Government, which was to rule until elections could be organised. Meanwhile, tens of thousands of workers and soldiers created a movement capable of running society for themselves through their own democratic councils, or soviets.

After the February Revolution, Reisner became involved with the writer Maxim Gorky's paper, *New Life*, which supported the new government. She also began teaching workers in the Provisional Government's spelling reform programme. 'It was Larissa's first experiences of meeting Petrograd's masses which formed her as a revolutionary and changed her life,' wrote her biographer Cathy Porter. In the sailors' clubs of Krondstadt, Reisner met the Bolshevik Fyodor Raskolnikov, whom she later married. During the summer months, the Provisional Government saw its power ebb away towards the workers' councils, which were based on workplace democracy rather than parliament. Demands for an end to the war and to social inequality fuelled support for the Bolshevik Party. In October, the Bolsheviks organised a revolution to transfer power to the workers and bring an end to the slaughter in the trenches.

Immediately after the October Revolution, Reisner went to the Bolshevik Central Committee to offer her services: 'I can ride, shoot, reconnoitre, write, send correspondence from the front, and, if necessary, die...' Larissa's first job for the new soviet government was to work with Anatoly Lunacharsky to issue an appeal to Petrograd's artists and cultural workers to attend a meeting to show support for the new regime. Only a handful turned up, but among them were three major figures in Russian culture, the poets Alexander Blok and Vladimir Mayakovsky and the theatre director Vsevolod Meyerhold. Larissa's second job was also alongside Lunacharsky, cataloguing works of art requisitioned from the collections of the wealthy on behalf of the worker's government.

In 1918, Larissa joined the Bolshevik Party as they planned the transformation of an under-developed Russia devastated by war. That endeavour was made even more difficult when the Civil War erupted in March 1918. Trotsky described the state of Russia in those weeks: 'At times, it seemed as if everything were slipping and crumbling, as if there were nothing to hold to, nothing to lean upon. One wondered if a country so despairing, so economically exhausted, so devastated, had enough sap left in it to support a new regime and preserve its independence. There was no food. There was no army. The railways were completely disorganized. The machinery of state was just beginning to take shape.' The embryonic workers' state came under attack by a coalition of imperial powers, united only by their bitter opposition to Bolshevism. In the west, German Armies occupied Poland, Lithuania, Latvia and a large area of Russia, and Austro-German troops occupied the Ukraine. There was a rebellion of fifty thousand Czech soldiers along the River Volga. German troops were approaching Moscow from the west, and anti-socialist White Russian armies were approaching Moscow from the east. The epicentre of the workers' state was caught between hammer and anvil. In the north, the French and English occupied Murmansk and Archangel, and threatened an advance on Vologda. As Trotsky wrote in the summer of 1918, 'The civil-war front was taking more and more the shape of a noose closing ever tighter about Moscow.' It was this desperate need to defend their revolution that led Larissa and thousands of other socialists, to volunteer for the Red Army.

Larissa Reisner became a political commissar in the army. In the summer of 1918, the strategically important city of Kazan fell to the Whites. Larissa was one of many who flocked to the area east of Moscow to stem the White tide. Trotsky described Larissa's activities: 'After the capture of Kazan by the Whites, she went into the enemy camp to reconnoitre, disguised as a peasant woman. But her appearance was too extraordinary, and she was arrested. While she was being cross-examined by a Japanese intelligence officer, she took advantage of an interval to slip through the carelessly guarded door and disappear. After that, she engaged in intelligence work.' Larissa's own descriptions of her undercover work are thrilling and imbued with socialist responses to the conduct of war. The Red Army rallied to make a stand at nearby Sviyazhsk under the leadership of Leon Trotsky. Larissa described the significance of the battle in 'Dispatches from the Frontline', one of the articles translated here: 'Today, it's a legend, one of those revolutionary legends which nobody has recorded yet but which is constantly retold in every corner of Russia. Not a single soldier who ever fought in the Red Army, nor the veterans from the foundation of the Workers and Peasants Army, returning home and reflecting on three years of Civil War, will fail to recall the epic story of Sviyazhsk, the place from which a wave of revolutionary offensives was set in motion which reached into every corner of Russia.' At Sviyazhsk thousands of political activists like Larissa played a crucial role in agitating among the war-weary regular troops to encourage them and motivate them to continue fighting. Larissa felt that they put 'backbone into the soft body of the army'.

In 1919 Larissa was a commissar at the Naval Headquarters in Moscow. On her return to Petrograd in 1920, she wrote the hugely popular *Letters from the Front*, which distilled her experiences of the frontline and the commitment of workers and peasants which enabled the workers' state to beat back the threat of the White Armies. She wrote in a new, direct, literary style which she saw as intimately linked to the revolutionary experience:

> To fight for three years, to march with guns for thousands of miles, to chew bread made with straw, to die, rot and shake with terror on a filthy bed in some flearidden hospital, and to conquer! Yes, to conquer the enemy who is three times stronger than we are, armed with our clapped-out rifles, our collapsing planes and our fourth-rate gasoline, while all the time wretched, angry letters arrive for our loved ones at home… For all this, I think we need a few verbal outbursts, don't you?

One review of *Letters from the Front* praised the way in which 'The author has, with exceptional talent, described how people made the Revolution, and how the Revolution made them'. The working men and women of Russia transformed themselves as they fought to transform their society.

Reisner and her husband were posted to Afghanistan in 1921 and lived there for two years. Reisner was given responsibility for winning Afghanistan to the Russian cause. This posting offered the possibility of a life of ease and glamour, but, according to Karl Radek, she chose instead to spend many hours studying British imperialism and Indian resistance. She developed from a Russian revolutionary into an international socialist campaigner. In 1923, she travelled illegally into Germany where she witnessed the abortive German Revolution of 1923. She published three important collections of articles about the German Revolution, *Berlin, October 1923*, *Hamburg at the Barricades* and *In Hindenburg's Country*. She also began a relationship with Karl Radek. In one article Larissa lambasted German arms manufacturers Krupps, recalling how in 1913, Krupp said, 'A factory must make its own demand.. Krupp made guns and war was his customer. In 1914 it broke out... No one was so enriched by the war as Krupp.' In another article, titled 'Milk', Larissa describes the hardships endured by working-class families and the Communist beliefs such conditions generated among the women. Her article revealed that Larissa did not observe the working classes from afar – she shared their grievances and their lives.

When she returned to Russia in 1924, Larissa took part in heated debates about how and why the German Revolution had failed. Aino Kuusinen was the wife of Otto Kuusinen, who was the secretary of the Comintern, an international association of socialist organisations. She described a dispute that broke out when visitors gathered in her husband's flat:

There was another knock: this time it was Karl Radek, whom I knew, accompanied by a very good-looking woman. He introduced her; the name meant nothing to me. A third knock, Bela Kun appeared... A furious argument began between him and Ernst Thälmann, each accusing the other...I sat on the sofa with Radek's friend, while the two men remained standing and continued to argue fiercely. I was amazed that they did so in the presence of an outsider, for the young woman did not belong to the Comintern and I had no notion why she was there. Radek was calm at first, but suddenly he joined in the quarrel and all three men shouted at once... Suddenly, to my astonishment, the woman jumped up and stood between Radek and Thalmann, shaking her fist at the latter and calling him a brainless prize-fighter and other uncomplimentary things... Suddenly the woman flew at Thalmann, tugging at his coat and hammering with her fists... To Otto, when they left our apartment, I said, 'Isn't it disgraceful of the men to go on like that in front of an outsider.' He replied, 'She's not an outsider – she's Radek's friend, Larissa Reissner.'

Larissa travelled across Russia, exploring the lives and political ideas of the working classes. In the Ural Mountains she described the hard life led by miners. She also continued to develop herself politically by preparing lectures on the 1905 Revolution to give to Party cells in industrial plants. Her writings were widely read and celebrated throughout Soviet Russia during the 1920s. We will never know what Larissa Reisner might have accomplished, because she died of typhus in February 1926, aged just 30. Neither do we know how she would have responded to the rise of Stalin. We do know that she worked closely with Leon Trotsky, both in the Red Army and in the last years of her life in the Commission for the Improvement of Industrial Products.

★ The articles published here as *Dispatches from the Frontline* represent an important contribution to our understanding of the Russian Revolution, the Civil War and the role of women in sustaining the Revolution and defeating its enemies. In the introduction, 'By the Author', Larissa describes the creativity unleashed by the revolutionary struggle against the White Armies, a military effort which depended for its success on the commitment and energy of the working classes. In 'Kazan' Larissa describes the experience of military defeat as Kazan was taken by the White Army. She writes powerfully about danger, escape, heroism and mundanity. Civil wars, she tells us, are won or lost by the state of the roads. At each stage of her dramatic escape from enemy troops, Larissa depended on the practical and emotional support of ordinary people. An apparently inexorable tide of defeats inflicted upon the Red Army was turned in the battle of Sviyazhsk. If Sviyazhsk had fallen, nothing would have stood between Moscow and the White Armies. In 'At Sviyazhsk' Trotsky writes, 'for a whole month, the fate of the Revolution hung again in the balance'. In 'Sviyazhsk', Larissa describes the arrival of Leon Trotsky at the town's train station and his immediate impact on the way the Red Army began to organise: the Red Army and the Revolution merged into one united force. Larissa observed the boring but incredibly tense wait for the military offensive to be launched: 'Morning, daytime, evening, night – every hour is long drawn out, it has to be endured and then outlasted, persevered until the very last second – much in the same way as every slice is sparingly and neatly cut right to the heel of an old loaf of bread. Every hour seemed precious, not at all like their previous lives – it was barely perceptible now, conjured up as a kind of miracle. It was a miracle.' The proximity of death infused every moment with a vivid sense of potential joy and meaning.

Larissa's writings describe battles on land and at sea, but hers is no conventional military history, it is a history of how ordinary men and women forged an army capable of defeating some of the most powerful armies in Europe. In 'From Kazan to Sarapul', Larissa describes a battle on the River Volga, during which the Red Army disguised themselves as White troops in order to launch a surprise attack. 'Markin' is preoccupied with another gunboat battle, this one on the River Kama. In the article, Larissa describes the death of the commander of the best of the gunboats, *Vanya-Communist*, in a confrontation from which she was lucky to escape. 'The Summer of 1919' focuses on a sea battle and introduces a range of revolutionary military leaders including the indefatigable whirlwind Vladimir Azin. Larissa draws on their stories to meditate on the relationship between the individual and the masses in bringing about historical change.

Dispatches from the Frontline is tremendously rich in historical detail, infused with a sense of political urgency. It is a unique record of revolutionary warfare, written by a poet and journalist at the height of her literary and political powers. She knew what it was to live under fire, to be woken by the sound of enemy bombs falling, and her narrative weaves together dramatic action, political insight and lyrical beauty:

That the old order has collapsed, that life grapples with bare hands for its irrefutable truth, for the white swans of its resurrection, for something invisible, bigger and better even than this segment of starry sky, visible through a window like velvet but with broken glass – towards the future of all mankind. Once a century they touch and change with living blood. Words like this, such harshly beautiful words – and the smell of the living sweat, the living breath of others sleeping side by side on the floor'.

Larissa's fight for the Revolution was literary, political and military.

It is a sad irony that today it is much easier to find the words of the men who paid tribute to this revolutionary woman writer than it is to find her own words. This volume helps to address this literary and political injustice. Larissa wrote little about the specific battles faced by women. As Cathy Porter explains, 'Larissa Reisner came of age at a time when it finally seemed possible for women to overstep the conventional female ethic of submission, renunciation and domesticity. Her writings vibrate with the power and challenge of women's life in the Revolution, and of the limitless possibilities, uncertainties and dangers opening up for them.' Larissa Reisner was able to assume a role in public life and in military affairs which would have been unthinkable to women of the previous generation, who were forced to live in the underground movement, in constant fear of arrest, imprisonment and exile. The Revolution transformed what was possible for thousands of Russian women.

One of the men who did pay tribute to Larissa was Leon Trotsky who writes:

Larissa Reisner was herself prominent in the Fifth army, as well as in the Revolution as a whole. This fine young woman flashed across the revolutionary sky like a burning meteor, blinding many. With her appearance of an Olympian goddess, she combined a subtle and ironical mind and the courage of a warrior... Her sketches about the civil war are literature. With equal gusto, she would write about the Ural industries and the rising of the workers in the Ruhr. She was anxious to know and to see all, and to take part in everything. In a few brief years, she became a writer of the first rank. But after coming unscathed through fire and water, this Pallas of the Revolution suddenly burned up with typhus in the peaceful surroundings of Moscow, before she was even thirty.

Her lover and comrade Karl Radek paid his own tribute to the power and importance of her literary legacy: 'Her one theme is the October Revolution. As long as people fight, think and feel and as long as they are drawn to find out "what it was like" they will read those books and will not put them down until they have reached the last page for they the smell of revolution about their breath.' This new translation of her works will bring the Revolution to life for a new generation of socialists.

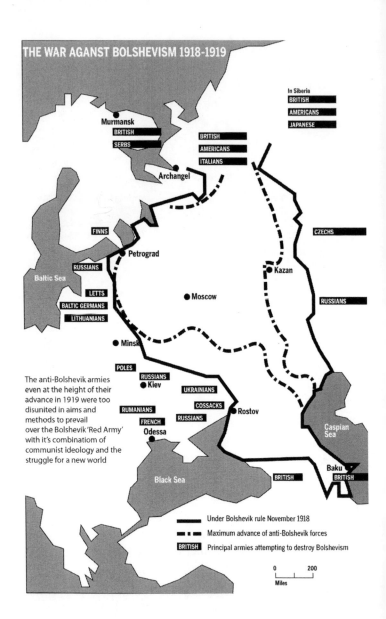

THE WAR AGANST BOLSHEVISM 1918-1919

In Siberia
BRITISH
AMERICANS
JAPANESE

BRITISH
SERBS

Murmansk

BRITISH
AMERICANS
ITALIANS

Archangel

CZECHS

FINNS

Petrograd

Kazan

RUSSIANS

Baltic Sea

LETTS
BALTIC GERMANS
LITHUANIANS

Moscow

RUSSIANS

Minsk

POLES
RUSSIANS
Kiev

The anti-Bolshevik armies
even at the height of their
advance in 1919 were too
disunited in aims and
methods to prevail
over the Bolshevik 'Red Army'
with it's combinatiom of
communist ideology and the
struggle for a new world

UKRAINIANS

RUMANIANS
FRENCH
Odessa

COSSACKS
RUSSIANS
Rostov

Caspian
Sea

Baku
BRITISH

Black Sea

BRITISH

—— Under Bolshevik rule November 1918

▬ ▬ Maximum advance of anti-Bolshevik forces

BRITISH Principal armies attempting to destroy Bolshevism

0   200
Miles

❂ THE WAR AGAINST THE BOLSHEVIKS

In his memoir, *My Life,* Trotsky wrote that the spring and summer of 1918 were unusually hard. All the aftermath of the war was beginning to make itself felt: millions had died in the conflict, epidemics of cholera, dysentery and typhus were raging, the army had disintegrated and troops had deserted in their droves: 'One wondered if a country so despairing, so economically exhausted, so devastated, had enough sap left in it to support a new regime and preserve its independence.'

Already, in September 1917, the British military attaché in Petrograd, Brigadier-General Alfred Knox, had supported an attempt by the Commander-in-Chief of the Russian army, General Kornilov, to mount an armed coup and establish a military dictatorship. This failed miserably but in early 1918, after the October Revolution, forces of the Triple Entente, led by Britain, invaded Russia. Their aim was to capture Moscow and, as Winston Churchill put it; 'to strangle Bolshevism in its cradle'.

On the Volga, in the summer of 1918, agents of Britain and

France had engineered a rebellion among the Czecho-Slovak regiments, made up of former war prisoners. By the time of the events described by Larissa Reisner in her dispatches from the frontline, the city and naval base of Kazan had already been taken and the extent of the territory under the control of the new Bolshevik government had been reduced to the size of the ancient principality of Muscovy: 'It had hardly any army; it was surrounded by enemies on all sides.'

After the taking of Kazan, it was only a short step to Nizhny-Novgorod and then a practically unobstructed road to Moscow. Leader of the forces opposed to the Bolsheviks – a loose amalgam of rival factions which became known as the Whites – was an Admiral in the Imperial Russian navy and formerly renowned polar explorer, Alexander Kolchak. During the Civil War he established an anti-communist government in Siberia and declared himself 'Supreme Leader and Commander-in-Chief of All Russian Land and Sea Forces'.

Kolchak was entirely dependent on the British. The Foreign Office hoped that, with their support, he could best assist the Allied cause by overthrowing Lenin and the Bolsheviks and bringing Russia back into the war on the side of the Allies. During the period from October 1918 to 1919, the British shipped an estimated 600,000 rifles, 6,831 machine guns and about 200,000 uniforms to assist Kolchak's counter revolutionary forces.

After seizing power in Siberia, in a British-sponsored *coup d'état*, Kolchak instituted a reign of terror which included mass floggings, mass executions and the extermination of whole villages. In the province of Irkutsk, one White commander (General Rozanov) issued an edict which stated, 'Those villages whose population meets troops with arms, burn down the villages and shoot the adult males without exception. If hostages are taken in cases of resistance to government troops, shoot the hostages without mercy.'

When Kolchak's forces reached Omsk: 'At least 2,500 people were killed. Entire carts of bodies were carried to the city, like winter lamb and pork carcasses.' In September 1918, during the suppression of peasant uprisings in Slavgorod, the Cossack warlord Annenkov, tortured and killed 500 villagers; the village of Black Dole was set ablaze, peasants were shot and hanged on pillars along with their wives and children, and girls from Slavgorod and surrounding areas were brought to Annenkov's train, raped and then shot.

In the summer of 1919, at the Adrianovsky station in the Transbaikal, more than 1,600 people were shot in a campaign of mass terror and executions. Eleven permanent death houses were set up where refined forms of torture were practised. According to the commander of the US occupation forces in Siberia, Major General Willian S Graves, 'White forces – under the protection of Japanese troops, were, '… roaming the country like wild animals, killing and robbing the people…If questions were asked about these brutal murders, the reply was that the people murdered were Bolsheviks and this explanation, apparently, satisfied the world.'

According to Major Graves, 'There were horrible murders committed, but they were not committed by Bolsheviks as the world believes. I am well on the side of safety when I say that the anti-Bolsheviks killed one hundred people in Eastern Siberia, to every one killed by the Bolsheviks.'

The White Army was generally responsible for the most active propaganda campaign against Jews, whom they openly associated with communism. Kolchak's successor as leader of the Whites, Anton Denikin, regularly incited violence against communist Jews and Jews seen as communists. A proclamation issued by one of Denikin's generals incited people to arm themselves in order to extirpate 'the evil force which lives in the hearts of Jew communists'.

John Ernest Hodgson, a British war correspondent with Denikin's forces, wrote that:

I had not been with Denikin more than a month before I was forced to the conclusion that…the officers and men of the Army laid practically all the blame for their country's troubles on the Hebrew. They held that the whole cataclysm had been engineered by some great and mysterious secret society of international Jews, who, in the pay and at the orders of Germany, had seized the psychological moment and snatched the reins of government. All the figures and facts that were then available appeared to lend colour to this contention.

According to Hodgson:

No less than 82 per cent of the Bolshevik Commissars were known to be Jews, the fierce and implacable 'Trotsky' - who shared an office with Lenin - being a Yiddisher whose real name was Bronstein. Among Denikin's officers this idea was an obsession of such terrible bitterness and insistency as to lead them into making statements of the wildest and most fantastic character. Many of them had persuaded themselves that Freemasonry was, in alliance with the Jews, part and parcel of the Bolshevik machine, and that what they had called the diabolical schemes for Russia's downfall had been hatched in the Petrograd and Moscow Masonic Lodges.

On 7 May 1918, the 8th Party Council of the Socialist Revolutionary (SR) Party convened in Moscow. It decided to start an uprising against the Bolsheviks with the aim of restoring the Constituent Assembly (which had been superceded by the Soviets). While these preparations were underway, the Czechoslovak Legions - who sided with the Entente powers during the war – had successfully overthrown Bolshevik rule in Siberia, the Urals and the Volga Region. This prompted the leadership of the SRs to focus on the Eastern Front.

On 8 June 1918, five members of the Constituent Assembly formed an All-Russian Constituent Assembly Committee in Samara and declared it to be the new Supreme Authority in the country. The committee had the support of the Czechoslovak Legions – but not of all Czechs, many of whom joined the Bolsheviks.

This short-lived alliance between the SRs and the Czech Legions is the one which had taken control of Kazan in the earliest of Larissa Reisner's dispatches. During the attack on Sviyazhsk witnessed by Larissa Reisner, two of the White generals in charge were Vladimir Kappel and Boris Savinkov. Kappel was a former Tsarist officer and a self-declared monarchist who was prepared to fight under any banner against the Bolsheviks.

Savinkov's background was quite different: he had been one of the leaders of the Fighting Organisation of the Socialist Revolutionary Party and had taken part in the Assassination of several high-ranking Tsarist officials during the 1905 Revolution.

In 1917, he was appointed Assistant War Minister during the period from July to August by Kerensky's Provisional Government. After the October Revolution, he became one of the most effective organisers of the armed resistance against the Bolsheviks. Savinkov was known to be an acquaintance of the legendary British spy Sidney Reilly, and was involved in a number of counter revolutionary plots against Bolsheviks, often in conjunction with the British Secret Intelligence Service (SIS).

Mayakovsky: Photo by Rodchenko

✪ LEFT MARCH

(Address to the Sailors)

All hands on deck –
About turn!
Now's no time for frivolities.
Quiet please, you orators!
Time for a word
From Comrade Mauser*.
Way too long, we've stuck to doctrines,
Passed down since the days of Adam & Eve.
We'll scrap this nonsense - pure make-believe.
Left!
Left!
Left!

Hey, you Navy Blues!
Right you are!
Time to take to the open waves!
Or, do the super-sharp keels
Of your men-o'-war
No long cut it?!
No matter, even if the great British Lion
Should emit an imperial roar.
It holds no fear for the Commune.
Left!
Left!
Left!

There, beyond
Mountains of woe
Awaits a new world, bathed in light.
Beyond the curse

Of famine and plague
The march of millions
Will put things right!
So, even if their war-dogs encircle,
Or a torrent of steel swirls round your head, –
Russia will never stoop to the Entente.**
Left!
Left!
Left!

Will the eagle's eyesight ever fail?
Need we always dwell
Upon what's gone?
Take a grip
On the world
By its throat
With your proletarian fist!
Chests out! Do or die!
Raise your banners to the sky!
Who will march to the right? Not I!
Left!
Left!
Left!

Vladimir Mayakovsky, 1918

New translation by Jack Robertson 2020

*Mauser: German semi-automatic pistol
** Alliance formed between Britain, France, Italy, Japan, the USA and Russia (until October 1917) in the war with Germany and Austria.

New translation by Jack Robertson 2020

DISPATCHES FROM THE FRONTLINE ✪ Larissa Reisner

By the author
Kazan
Sviyazhsk
From Kazan to Sarapul
Markin
The Summer of 1919

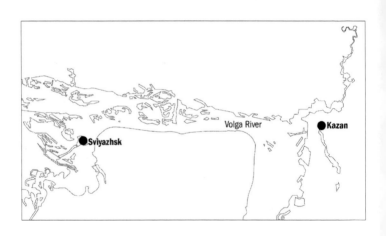

✪ BY THE AUTHOR

There are a few dirty, sprawling, cavernous buildings in Moscow where thousands of young soldiers, workers and peasants go to study. It's not a pleasant environment in these jam-packed dormitories, where the air in the lecture halls is thicker, damper and more foetid than the kind that old students would breathe as they shuffled through the endless sunlit corridors of my *alma mater*, Petersburg University.[1] But these are an entirely new breed, charged with the mantra of steering: 'Left! Left! Left!'.[2] In just a few short years, they need not only to grasp the best and most essential elements of the new ideological tenets at breakneck speed but be able to impart them to others. These new entrants to the Workers' Faculty, or *Rab-Fak*,[3] will be tomorrow's judges and their heirs and successors in the coming decade.

The Revolution is frantically wearing out its professional workers. It's a merciless task-master. You can't talk to it about an eight-hour working day, about protecting motherhood and raising wages. It demands everything - your brain, will-power, nervous energy, your life. As soon as it has drained you to the last drop, you are cast aside, worn-out and shattered, while it enlists a new supply of exceptional combatants from the inexhaustible reserve of the masses.

A few more years of this - from the assault columns proclaiming a social revolution in October of the great year, from the fighting near St Petersburg and Kazan, near Yaroslavl, Warsaw, Perekop in the Crimea and the Prikapisky desert of Kazakhstan, in Siberia and the Urals, near Arkhangel and in the Far East - there will be almost no one left. This entire layer will end up as fertilizer, as engine oil, as coal and oil for the All-Russian furnace.

And the new proletarian culture, our glorious new beginning, will not be created by the soldiers and commanders of the Revolution, nor by its defenders and heroes, but by the completely new cohort of very young people, who now - sitting in the stale, stuffy classrooms of the Workers' Faculty - digest science and risking their last kopek and their proletarian backsides to absorb Marx, Ilyich (Lenin) and Trotsky.

These students are an unbridled, irreconcilable nation of materialists. From their life experience, from their worldview, with calm courage, they have thrown out all the conformity of patterns and seeming symmetrical beauty, the sweetness, comforts and mystical consolations of bourgeois science, and its aesthetics, art and mysticism. Talk to the students in the Workers' Faculty about 'beauty' and they will take it as a terrible insult. Mention creativity or feelings, they'll smash up the chairs and leave the hall. Quite right too.

Nonetheless - you youngsters, you children of the proletariat - make sure that while you are mocking and deriding the bourgeois sentiments, you do not fall into the trap which has survived perfectly well for many years and snapped old strings. Its rusty old jaws can still snap into action. If bourgeois-individualist love, caprice and inspiration are not for you, then remember that the immortality of those who have just departed and their lasting influence has only now been called into question, amid the typhus, starvation and rampant fever of these wasted years.

Don't be taken in by the Apollonian aesthetes (of reason, culture, harmony and restraint), the sophisticated connoisseurs and lovers of Russian verbosity, who frowned in disgust at the majestic, naked figure of Venus. They like to peg their noses against the Revolution. They shun the use of what they regard as such gauche, unseemly terms as - 'heroism' – 'brotherhood of nations' – 'self-denial' – 'fight to the bitter end'! And not only talking about these rough-and-beautiful things but actually going out and doing them will immediately make a man of an educated upbringing begin to feel a knot in the pit of his stomach!

Take this example: a fleet of ships, several dozen iron-clad barges and tugs, twenty thousand sailors from Kronstadt and the Black Sea, all mustered at the Revolution's command. To fight for three years, to march thousands of miles from the Baltic to the Persian border, to survive on bread bulked out with straw, to die, to fester and tremble with fever on louse-ridden, filthy mattresses in poverty-stricken hospitals. To win, finally, to defeat, with the strongest of our own, and to vanquish the second strongest armies of our enemies. Can we do it with shot guns, and with planes which fall from the sky and break down every day and are smashed to smithereens because of second-rate gasoline and all the while getting desperate, evil messages from the rear? It's an absolute nightmare. It was necessary to have a response.

What do you think? Should we simply have manufactured words in order to overcome the innate, inescapable cowardice of human flesh, its blood, its thin skin, which can be ripped

Inside the Rab-Fak

open by as little as a rusty nail? It doesn't take much to start the bleeding – the lifeblood flows out so easily and it's all over. I needed to see beyond the gore and the filth, beyond the monotonous queues at the Department of Social Security, where the exhausted receptionist you meet in the entrance hall can't even provide you with an artificial leg to replace the one that's been blown off.

Tomorrow it could be a sailor on one of the *Karl Liebknecht* [4] destroyers, bearing aloft a red banner, who spills his ration of porridge all over the deck when it's smashed into by a shell. And what about dying? What happens without the high priests of God and Satan, without all their comforting lies, all done away with by the Revolution? There's only just time to say 'here are my boots – you take them' and that's the end of that.

Whether it's beauty or not, it's a magnificent thing to see when an ambush on a ship destroys an emplacement and the commander yells from the bridge at the panic-stricken crew in such a way that they nevertheless peel themselves up from the decks and rush to their guns: 'Stern gunners, I order you in the name of the Republic – open fire.' And the stern gunners unleash a broadside?

And creativity also belongs to us, it's not just a bourgeois trait. For instance, we needed to blow up some exceptionally well-equipped ships supplied by the British, for the superbly armed White Fleet. So, unknown to anyone, a communist engineer, Brzezinski, invented a brilliant thing: he worked out how to fix mines to the keels of ordinary sailing boats and in that way was able to arm a whole flotilla of sailboats. Of course, there are some people who are ready to take on this type of desperate task. The fact that some attempts do not succeed is not down to the failure of an apprentice fisherman, comrades. When that very old communist Popov died, we would no longer see his long frock-coat, bright gaiters and white cheerful Spitz – the dog that followed him everywhere – either at the Cheka or at the Fleet HQ. He died amazingly, under torture, but said nothing. Revolutionary psychology or not?

I dedicate this book to the students of the Workers Faculty. Let them curse, and let some other supposedly heretical words lodge in their throats.

'They loved.'

'Died well.'

'Revolutionary psychology.'

But let them read to the end how it really was, from Kazan to Enzeli, the roar of victory, the pain of defeat. On the Volga, on the River Kama and on the Caspian Sea during the Great Russian Revolution. That's all.

✪ KAZAN

The city has not yet been taken, but its defeat is certain. The doors of rooms which have just been abandoned swing back and forth on their hinges. Everywhere the floors are covered with discarded papers and other abandoned, disjointed, random belongings. There's nothing worse than a retreat. From all corners, the blurred faces of inconspicuous neighbours not seen for many months start to materialise. Some wear buttons with a shabby lustre, something that looks like a cockade, or even a service ribbon – but it is still hard to make out, in the half-dark of the getaway corridors. Too faint-hearted to shout out a frantic 'We surrender!'.

In front of the porch the vague outline of an emplacement can be made out: dusty, intense, malevolent faces, abrupt commands, and somewhere on a nearby bridge the rumble of wheels and the clatter of cavalry. The last resistance is being prepared; they're getting ready for the final assault. Windows rattle as the lorries pass by – the noise they make kills off their last hope. They are afraid.

At doors decorated with superfluous whitewashed signs saying things like *Operations* and *Secretariat* a few women say goodbye to their loved ones, while behind them some impudent flunkeys sweep away the revolutionary detritus from beautiful red rugs. The dust swirls up, roused by their defiant brush strokes. That's how the bitterness and taint of defeat is swept from the doorway in the wake of our recent footsteps, by a janitor's brushstroke.

It's a strange feeling to be moving about in an unfamiliar building with windows and doors slammed shut knowing full well that a battle to the death is about to take place in this godforsaken hotel. It's a racing certainty that someone will be killed, some will survive, some will be taken prisoner. At such moments, all the words and all the rationalisations that help preserve your presence of mind go out the window. All that remains is an acute, penetrating sorrow - and underneath it, barely perceptible, a disorienting question: whether to flee or stand your ground. In the name of what? Face screwed up, choking with tears, the heart reiterates: stay calm, don't panic, no humiliating exodus.

But as soon as the first mortar bomb smacks into the ground nearby, in a swampy meadow next to the Kazan Kremlin, and one lands slap-bang in the headquarters – which is where the last of us to leave are holed up - it's now become impossible to continue, all restraint goes to pieces, we must pull back.

I'm weighed down with important papers and something else which is top-secret, with an order to take them with us and hand them over to the next HQ staff we come across. I've got to ignore the barrage of shells now pounding into the white cornice of Hotel Siberia. I try not to think about the hotel retainers sweeping up the clouds of dust, or about the armoured car and the terrible pot-holed road we're heading along. Will we ever make it?

Next to us a family with children runs along carrying samovars; not far ahead a woman is tugging at the rope attached to a frightened goat. She's got a baby in her arms. Everywhere you look, all along the golden autumn fields, is an endless stream of poor folk, soldiers, wagons piled high with domestic goods and chattels, all with the self-same fur coats, blankets and utensils.

I remember how much easier it became once we had joined this tide of humanity. Who are these fugitives? Are they Communists? Unlikely. A woman with a goat probably doesn't have a party card. Every time a shot is fired or there's an explosion, a terrible panic ensues, scattering the crowd, all of whom make the sign of the cross towards each and every bell-tower we pass. It's simply a mass of ordinary people trying to save themselves from an old enemy. It's as though the whole of Russia, which knows all about the yolk on its shoulders, is trudging away from its Czecho-Slovakian[5] 'liberators' on this muddy highway.

Outside the city, the stream of fugitives begins to thin out. Women and children, with their guides, continue to move straight ahead, without turning around or deviating from the route, driven on by a powerful collective instinct. Some individuals stride along in the torrential rain with no coat or hat, a few are desperately clutching their briefcases. They curl around on the sideways track or head directly through uncharted steppe, stumbling, falling and getting up again until they reach remote villages by nightfall.

The summer rain has turned into a downpour, the fields have turned black and become an unremitting hard slog. The heavy cloud that looms over Kazan is lifting. By now the city has been taken. The thunder of gunfire has ceased. Under the ominous sky, campfires silently flicker and lightning flashes in the distance. A menacing cloud of carrion-crows circles over the suburbs.

How many of us there were, and where we went, I don't remember. Every step we took on what we thought was the way to Sviyazhsk was held up by ploughed fields of sodden wet clay.[6] At the time of our retreat, especially in the first few hours, much depended on a vague hunch – being forced to choose between one of three villages or just one of a number of directions. All of the senses were intensified – the glance of a passer-by, the silhouette of a tree, the bark of a dog; everything took on the appearance of danger. Either that, or a calm conviction that 'it's possible'.

Ahead of us all, with his bald head, and in a soaking wet but absurdly respectable jacket, marched the pen-pusher supposedly in charge, Comrade B, known to the rest of us as Portfolio. He understood nothing about the subtle indicators along our route – his powers of observation were non-existent; he was slow on the uptake. Most of all, he wanted just to lie down and fall asleep after the last few nerve-shredding nights in the city.

Our real leader was a diminutive seaman: with his little bandy legs, he effortlessly negotiated the clumps of clay, the rain didn't prevent him from seeing things with his one, jaunty blue eye and most of all he always stayed calm. To contend with 'Portfolio', who was forging ahead without thinking, at the same time as having to take into account the wind and fatigue, he abruptly veered left and took a detour of practically ten kilometres in order to bypass the first village, behind which we found a proper road, neon-lit in the darkness. That way took us to the second village. Our commander ordered us to come to a halt and knocked on the door of a dingy log cabin. We slept on the floor, delighted to get the heavy, wet boots off our feet. Bales of hay, bodies crammed together, a lamp in the corner.

Half-asleep, time to discard all the poisonous thoughts, with another hunk of warm black bread. In the morning it turned out that the entire room was full of refugees, which none of us had realised. A bit of bad-mouthing began, with each person standing their ground and accentuating their own predicament.

Our supposedly 'responsible' man-in-charge – the one we called Portfolio – with all the naivety of a genuine city-dweller and intellectual with it, decided to intervene with an inscrutable disguise: his impenetrable incognito. The hat he'd been wearing had somehow been ripped and suddenly disappeared, only to be replaced by a desperate-looking cap which immediately made him look like a convict.

It so happened that the owner of our shelter was a village teacher. He very much wanted to adopt the tone of master, but there were so many of the stricken and they were such a sorrowful sight that he kept it to just one moral adage. Generally speaking, he was a kindly soul who cooked for everyone free of charge and honestly told us the way to Sviyazhsk. He even accompanied us to the path, waving his arms and getting excited – though we did argue a bit about the Court of Justice. It was this teacher's path that saved us: on the main road, which most of the refugees had taken, an ambush was already waiting.

Sviyazhsk – why do they call it Sviyazhsk? The name of this small staging post on the banks of the River Volga – which subsequently played such a crucial role in the defence of and then the taking back of Kazan – is known as the anvil upon which the nucleus of the Red Army was forged, rose up and then was repeated. It has become a spontaneous by-word for fortitude in the midst of panic and retreat. Whether or not HQ chose Sviyazhsk as the best place to consolidate its position or chose this name to symbolise a collective instinct for self-preservation, it's the automatic inspiration whenever retreat or failure beckons.

✪

A Civil War is pretty much won or lost on the main roads. Now and then, it's worth turning off onto a country road, along a lane, rushing through its pleasant, sweet scented hedgerows and back to the embrace of peace, autumn and the perfect tranquillity of the last days of summer. We made our way barefoot, with our boots and a hunk of bread dangling from canes over our shoulders. Our sailor-in-charge picked up a long shepherd's crook from somewhere and prodded Portfolio in the back with it, until he eventually slumped to the ground and was ready to burst into tears.

No, I must confess that our Comrade B.V. hardly ever took us into the villages and when he did, it was usually one run by the Old Believers.[7] They always keep the place clean, sympathise with our cause, the milk they have is as sweet as in the Kingdom of Heaven, and the women have the complexion of fresh honey. Not once did the Old Believers let us down or let us go hungry.

On the third day, practically nothing happened. Portfolio

managed to hurt his leg somehow, got tired and whined. Two of my seafaring comrades had already had enough of trekking on dry land, swallowing the dust and generally trying to act as land-lubbers so that their combined groaning even began to have an effect on the unflappable Mishka (the Bear – the nickname of our guide).

Then, suddenly, our state of bliss was interrupted. From out of nowhere, up popped a squire in a blue, cotton tunic with a red sash and with a beard *a la Rus* – looking either like a solitary Cossack or a militant landowner. Our reluctant captain took one look at him sideways and turned even greyer and more subdued. The stranger's inquisitive eyes darted from Portfolio to his attaché case, to Mishka calmly drinking tea, and then to the very matter-of-fact, even more easy-going sailors.

And so began the most wary, cautious conversation between us.

'Are you refugees from Kazan?'

Our leader answered smartly on our behalf, 'No, we're searching for a dacha. We're looking for a place with a good view of the river and with all amenities…and generally comfortable. Would you be able to recommend one?' The old fellow's face was unshaven and stern – he's a thoroughbred southerner, thick-set, cheerful and direct. Standing there in his tunic, he chuckled, 'You're not making this up, are you? So, you haven't been kicked out of Kazan then? Well and truly booted out?' This was clearly a comrade, even Portfolio could grasp that immediately. 'You must be one of us, surely?' Then he gave us a wink – with a teardrop in his eye.

Mishka jolted into action. He blurted out the type of reinforcements needed by the Red Army, 'Lord help us, we could do with 20-inch guns from Kronstadt,[8] with ammunition ready for battle – within two or three days.' He stared intently at our new companion, then turned his attention sideways, out towards the open steppe. Far off in the distance, the silhouette of some riders could be made out, the peaks of their lances like black needles.

Our new friend looked uneasy but there was nothing to worry about: at this point Mishka cheerfully stuffed his hands into his pockets and we all took cover quickly through a garden and into a nearby field (with Portfolio lagging behind, of course). For the rest of the day, in the sultry heat, we slept among golden wheatsheaves, not far from the road. A few times, some Cossacks passed close by and at that point Comrade Ippodi woke Portfolio so that he wouldn't snore too loudly. It was quite a setting on a dark and stormy night. Endless flashes of lightning in the half-dark, the creaking of the wagons, the whinnying of the horses.

Hand-held lanterns danced about in the darkness. Exhausted and off-track, we eventually caught up with our convoy just minutes before it was ready to leave. Going where? To Sviyazhsk. We'll be part of the HQ staff, the surviving military unit, the workers from the Political Department. They recognise us. One of them comes up and looks at us in the unsteady light from a lantern. With great difficulty, as though I had sand or cotton-wool in my mouth, I ask him, 'Is Raskolnikov[9] with you?'. 'No.' He quickly lowers the lantern, so that the expression on his face is hidden in the darkness.

All night, the wagons stretch along a heavily rutted road in a downpour, accompanied by continuous blue tracers of rifle fire. One of the wagons gets stuck, the order is passed from one truck to the next, the entire convoy grinds to a halt. More running-around with lanterns, you can hear the heavy braying of the horses bogged down in a quagmire, and then we get going again with shuffling steps. The rain keeps on coming, an impenetrable pine forest creaks in the wind, and with every flash of lightning you can make out the murky shape of a peasant

Interior of Teplushka, *heated railway carriage equipped with wood-burning stove, used for troop-carrying.*

supporting the flank of his exhausted horse and somebody's white, exhausted face dripping wet from the thunderstorm. And then it stops.

There's no need to describe the morning of the following day in any detail: it was the same as every other day during our retreat. Snatches of sleep under bales of wet hay, aching in our worn-out legs, the remorseless banter of the soldiers, especially when they sharpen up, sitting on their backsides in the field kitchen – the place where we all go, in turn, to take a break.

The dogged, unwavering steps taken by the subdued wife of Comrade Raskolnikov.[10] She looks at nothing, listens to nothing and speaks to no one. Without turning around, the white handkerchief on her head stands out against a background of scythed autumn fields. She still doesn't know for sure if he's going to be dead or alive, but the sense of foreboding grows stronger by the minute – you can see how it takes hold of her, all the more harshly and cruelly. For a stranger, it's hard to take her bottled-up, confounded certitude.

Finally, we reach the Volga, a crossing, the station, a sleep on a cold floor, the hot stove of a Teplushka. Another twenty-four hours gone by on wet, desolate roads. Next morning, another push – the wheels squeal, the long-awaited, rousing jolt of the carriages – and, within an hour, we are actually in Sviyazhsk. But there's no sign of who we are looking for in Sviyazhsk. In the Commandant's Office, a flurry of questions and conversations.

Then, a clued-up Commandant suddenly appears and unthinkingly rubs salt in the wound: 'Nothing to worry about – he'll be OK. He's probably escaped to Paris.' A moment later he stands there, drenched in hot tea, red in the face, taken aback and angry, but it doesn't change anything. Everything is painted black, to every question the answer seems to disguise a peculiar, hidden agenda. Finally, a telegram arrives from Comrade Trotsky in which he says that Fyodor Fyodorovich had been taken prisoner by the Whites. The realisation dawns on my ashen, stony face: Raskolnikov has been killed, without a doubt.[11]

At that point, Misha and I decided to head back to Kazan. On a scrap of tissue paper, Comrade Bakinsky scribbled out a permit that would allow us pass through all of our checkpoints. And, knowingly winking with his one blue eye, he said, 'Look out for the Commander of the Latvian regiment – most likely he'll give you a couple of horses to take you up to the front line. From there, you can do the rest on foot.'

He was right, the Latvians did help - and so did an element of deceit: we had to pretend that Raskolnikov was also a Latvian. That was only partially true, on his mother's side. They sorted me out with a greatcoat, pants and boots and the cavalry provided us with two horses – but, for goodness sake, how is anybody meant to get saddled up on an excitable creature like this? Approach from the left or from the right? And what to do then with your legs, to which are attached – for good reason – a pair of massive stirrups? We headed off at walking pace – no problem. Then at a trot – anguish and fear. And we had got another forty miles of this ahead of us.

On the very first day of getting to know this chestnut beauty, an attachment developed which was to last for the next three years. Far beyond the Volga, right on the perimeter of the railway line, the horse suddenly bridled. I prodded him to go ahead but his ears quivered nervously and he glowered up at me with a hostile look – there was no way he was going to proceed. The cavalrymen who were with us also stopped, and laughed. Then, suddenly, right in front of our noses, one after another, the pillars of three thunderous explosions, three men dead. It was time to make for the forest.

Lots of trees had already been blown to bits – and shells were still whistling into the undergrowth with a screaming crunch. The trees stood silently, like condemned men – surprisingly still and upright.

In much the same way as anyone would laze quietly in a meadow, here in the midst of redolent, rusty-red pine trees. The soldiers and their two commanders went quiet as they approach their concealed emplacement. This was where they would eat. Pots of soup were steaming in the warm grass. Two or three men would eat from them together.

Talking in a whisper for some reason - no doubt worried about jeopardising this patch of the clearing - they questioned us and verified our documents before we were invited to eat with them. It was comical what their soup smelled of: thick, pale-green cabbage, swollen and puffed up in the boiling water together with wild strawberries, whose rosy blush was evident everywhere round here, in among the slender, parched grasses and herbs.

During the lull, somewhere out there in the forest, a filthy, sweaty, half-deaf artilleryman tries to locate our camouflaged shelter with the help of some arithmetic and his own shrewd, innate cunning. As we are taking a break, the stationary pine trees emit the spirit of the place and, somewhere nearby, a forest bird starts to chirrup uncertainly. Most likely, it's a blue-tit. Chirp, chirp, then silence.

The soldiers stop eating and listen out attentively. One of them picks up a frantic, industrious ant on his spoon and watches it dart about with rapt concentration. It's easier for all of us when another invisible projectile whizzes overhead, explodes in a thicket beyond and scatters white resinous splinters from the pine trees which have been hit. It's missed us though – and all the spoons can go back in the soup.

And so, once more, we move on, mesmerised by the motionless forest until we can make out some big empty buildings at its outer edge. Beyond them is the railway line - and something strange is happening. Individual railway carriages are strung out along the line, some in twos, some singly, at quite large distances from each other. It's as though they are playing a trick on us: turn one way and they come towards us; look back again and they are where they were when we first caught them unawares in their curious positions.

The carcasses of dead horses are scattered here and there and from time-to-time mortar shells explode all across this desolate, eerie place. The next HQ is nearby, in the building closest to the station. It's a hard thing to relate, but about an hour after our departure, it took a direct hit from the emplacement we were looking for, about five miles away. One of our best commanders, Comrade Yudin, was killed.

While he was still alive, he'd welcomed us and during the last few hours of his increasingly energetic life had been worked up like a vein that's full to bursting. We'd spent a few short, piquant moments with him, the air bursting with expletives. He looked at the documents, laid them in front of him on the table, told us to eat and gave us a bed. While we were resting and drinking tea, we could hear a telephone call to the Revolutionary Soviet in Sviyazhsk which was taking place in the room next door (you could hear everything through the walls of this building). 'Have you heard of somebody called Leisner? Yes - Leisner? Do we let them carry on? Yes? Very good. That's what we thought – very well, all the best.'

Anybody who finds themself in a bank for some reason will always start to feel like a thief. The bronze lattice-work, fireproof cash-registers, volumes of accounting books piled up, the impeccable sheen of the parquet floor, all the high-security, and lock-clicking politeness assumes that every visitor is either a bandit or a con-man.

For a moment, when the name of a certain R cropped up in the conversation, I suddenly felt that my behaviour must seem extremely unconvincing, my appearance very suspicious. Damn! What about my voice even? I'd said very plainly, 'I'm going to Kazan on top-secret business.' With a stranger's unfamiliar, deceitful voice. It's obvious: I must be a spy.

It was already twilight when Comrade Yudin came to our room. His face was barely visible, but his entire presence - the big, crumpled breeches, his riding spurs, his hands calmly stuffed in his pockets – all seemed affable. After quizzing us a bit more on where we were heading and how we intended to get there, he advised us to keep going, even though we'd already made up our minds on that dire folly. 'Well, best of luck', he said - I hope we meet again.' Then he shook our hands firmly, thinking to himself that we're not going to get out of this forest live. Behind his back, the Grim Reaper smiled sardonically into the darkness.

Glumly looking at his massive boots and trousers, I noticed that the Red Army adjutant who brought the tea was interested in them every bit as much as I was.

'Comrade, Ma'am – why don't we do a swop? You give me your munitions and I'll give you some proper ladies clothes – with ruffles and feathers?'. And with a flourish he produced from somewhere in the attic a Parisian corset, a pair of officer's trousers and, much to my delight, a dark, woman's suit.

The precious pair of officer's pants soon turned up covering the wiry backside of the dispatch runner and one of the Red Army soldiers tried out the pink corset. Misha and myself soon emerged from the masquerade looking so much the respectable bourgeois couple that at the very first checkpoint we came to we were arrested again – despite all the passwords, paperwork and permits we had with us. Furious, Misha travelled back to the HQ under escort and didn't return until it was already getting dark. As we left, the sentry gave some good advice: as far as possible, steer clear of the railway line and instead stick to the forest. 'Watch it', he warned - because the railway lines stand out clearly in the dark – 'they'll pinpoint you and finish you off in an instant'.

A few hours on a quiet country road. We met two scouts. They gave us a fright – and vice-versa. We chatted a little, appreciating the human contact, then carried on. The forest bathes the fatigue in legs exhausted by walking - like an immense, black lake. I still remember the stars, the fear of the darkness, the fear of being without a home, without a bed, with no tomorrow. It's more or less the usual, unsettled response of any townie separated from their comfort zone.

On some country lane or other, in some village or other, near some house or other, the despairing screams of a woman: a young Kyrgyz girl had been in labour for three days, in the bath, on the floor, and had not been able to give birth. We knocked on the door, unfamiliar faces, the touch of unknown hands probably helped to soothe her nerves, assisted her will to live – with a terrifying convulsion she pushed out the baby. Almost immediately, she calmed down, muttered a few babbling words through her sweat-drenched hair and fell asleep. Then I nodded off too, no longer clutching her dry, warm fingers like a little bird.

To cut a long story short, the young Kyrgyz woman went to the christening in a petticoat, the baby was carried to the church in a silk handkerchief and with a few pagan charms, in case it was ever abducted. We avoided going to the church. The priest, who was understanding of the old Mongol ways, sensed a more dangerous demonic force in the shape of the godparents who had just arrived.

After the christening, the happy father offered to take us to Kazan on his own horse, as a token of his gratitude.

'It's clear to see that you are good, decent people. I'm not still wet behind the ears and, thank goodness, I understand when a person can be trusted.'

'But if we were stopped at a checkpoint, what would you say?'

'I'd tell them you're summer visitors, heading home from your dacha. They know me well, they'd believe me.'

And true enough, on a warm morning, heavy with dew, a Kyrgyz cart transported us along quiet country lanes. When we reach the end, it was overgrown with bright, forest grass, you could hear the sound of woodpeckers drilling, there was the smell of resin and wild strawberries. From time to time, tearing through the pure morning air, the screaming descent of a mortar over our heads. Heavy artillery was pounding the forest.

Russian provinces are mostly pretty dilapidated, ugly and boring. All of the towns and villages are very similar to each other, like stale loaves of bread. But amid all this general ugliness, only a single structure in Kazan stands out which has style and architectural character and that is the Söyembikä Tower.[12]

Everything else, by comparison with this purely Tartar monument, is much more typically Mongolian. Watermelons, dust, buildings where there's nothing but a sign and a shop window and roadways made out of stone slabs and backbreaking blocks of granite. You need to cling to a slavish patriotism to have any affection for this side of Russia, in its bourgeois squalor, with its drab, monotonous, run-down and grubby appearance.

Not a single patrol stopped our horse and cart and we entered the Admiralty suburb, hardly believing our luck, although the uniform ugliness of the streets and houses all around was a sure sign to us that it was no longer a dream but very definitely Kazan, terror-stricken by the cock-eyed, impertinent ravings of the White Guards.

'So, exactly where are you taking us, chief – what happens now?'. Our Kyrgyz wagon driver turned towards us jauntily, smiling all over his roly-poly face. 'You need to be somewhere out of the way. There aren't many places like that here – I'll take you to the local Police Chief. He's his own man - I mean trustworthy and sympathetic. Me and him are old mates.' With that, he merrily snapped the reins on the horse's curved back. Misha and I just looked at each other, speechless. 'The Police Chief!'

The cart set off into a wide, dusty, suburban street. It had a wooden boardwalk, with tufts of grass sprouting through all its crevices. The houses were single-storey, with gates that squeaked and creaked, and all with green and white night-time shutters. In a word, the solid blue of an open sky, clouds rising like steam from a samovar, it was just like Maxim Gorky's *Town of Okurov*,[13] or the kind of bright and bold silken colours in a painting by Boris Kustodiev.[14] Our quick-witted driver brought the wagon to a halt in front of the most elegant house, kissed us goodbye and loyally handed us over to the Police Chief, who had come out onto the porch.

Misha and I immediately began to act the part: soon the elements of a harmless bourgeois comedy that you might see in a production put on by the Arts Theatre were being played

out in the upper rooms of the house we'd been delivered to –
with its spotlessly clean, beautifully waxed and polished floors,
with geraniums in the windows, icons in the corner and with
photographs of the District Courthouse above the writing desk.

In amongst the out-dated frock-coats and the high stiff
collars it was easy to make out the bulging eyes, high cheekbones
and smooth, flyblown forehead of our host.

Naturally, also sitting among the silent, neat rows in the
photo was the shrill wife of the Police Chief, with her evil, shiny
cranium. Their daughter, Pasha, pink and plump ('everything
in her tiny hands and eyes, in her eyes and tiny hands', as Gogol
would say) passed her time levering her ample breast over a low
window-sill and spitting out seeds at the occasional passer-by.

Like a flighty debutante, she never got involved in politics,
and only at the height of acute, hysterical, flagrant scandals –
equating her mother with the tenants on the lower floors – did
she get peeved, pucker her pink lips and say, 'Mummy, dear,
you are so ignorant, you have no right to speak so stridently.'

Downstairs, underneath the Police Chief, with his waxed
floor and geraniums, lived a few workers with their families
in corner flats. For a time, the Revolution interrupted the
simple and easily understood relationship between the upper
and lower floors; to the extent that there was no guarantee that
Pasha's trousseau would be complete.

The Police Chief's iron-grip, which had steadily, smugly
and patriarchally sapped the life-blood of the entire building,
suddenly found it was without sustenance and even experienced
a few manifest bites and injuries from 'downstairs'. It got
to the point that one of the tenants, a worker's family, had
requisitioned the Police Chief's fluffy, white goat for their
children.

But then, in July, the Lord above intervened in the sordid
business of ordinary mortals. Justice and the courts, exceeding

their limits, brandished the obsolete letter of the law, and the splendid Pasha was not in the least concerned or surprised when the violent tenant was led past her on the street, never to be seen again. After that, it was all back to normal: by comparison, the new rulers hauled the naked bodies of workers to the Volga in carts. From the Police Chief's house, idyllic phantoms fled.

The whole of his family could now resume sucking the life out of the 'downstairs' inhabitants – who were now frightened to cry or make any noise - quietly and happily slurping away. At a time like this, when the wrath of God, and even of the Czechs, was in full swing, we stayed here at the Police Chief's. At first, he appeared a little embarrassed to continue his old, everyday habit of starting his delicious meal with twitching hind legs in his mouth - like a hedgehog which is reluctant to eat a live frog in the middle of the day. But once he'd had a cup of tea with his guests, and denounced the Jews and the Communists, he became convinced of our political trustworthiness and completely relaxed.

To amuse himself, he went into town, not more than once every three days. The whole street and all of the 'downstairs' knew perfectly well that he'd be off again to denounce one or other of them at the HQ. That very evening, the police would come for the next victim, while, upstairs, they drank tea. Mummy dear listened intently to the commotion going on below.

Papa habitually and cheerily recognised that he and he alone was to blame – but, as a good Christian and an Officer to boot, he had no right to hide an offender etc. If only the Police Chief knew the toxic poison that his reasoning elicited on our nerves.

Pasha, all in pink calico and with her soul in a cloudless sky, where paper doves and forget-me-nots flutter, quietly poured a sixth cup of tea for the neighbour who was a teacher. Downstairs, they simply called him 'the Groom', investing this ardent name with intense hatred because of his unkempt beard, glasses and general intelligence.

And when the prolonged wailing began downstairs, Mummy dear chortled, like butter in a frying pan. Papa was genuinely astonished from behind his glasses, reading a page from a 1911 edition of *Modern Times.* Pasha listened with furrowed brow as the teacher explained to her what the Constituent Assembly[15] meant.

Next morning, Misha headed off to town to investigate, taking with him the money and his papers. The Police Chief set off on his rounds, to locate and confiscate weapons being concealed by the workers. Mummy dear sank into the sweetest abyss down in the basement, removing the scum from bitter and caustic grief, like cream from the milk, in the rotten darkness of this house. Papa settled down behind a novel by the inevitable Raoul. I read a newspaper. There wasn't a single name I recognised among the names of those who were reported to have been executed. In this way, all of the inhabitants of the Police Chief's house got on with their own business, quite independent of each other.

Big fat flies buzzed at the window-panes, everyone gently sank into a soporific daze. Within an hour, though, two rolls of thunder which had seemed much further away the day before, now resounded much closer to the city. Milky trails of shrapnel began to flare up and scatter across the silken sky, iridescent like a bolt of merchant's satin. The already sparsely populated streets now became completely abandoned, their usual lassitude now condensed into an ominous silence.

The Police Chief returned home agitated. While we were having lunch and he had only just started on a detailed description of his latest search, the first metal fragment crashed into the roof. The family was alarmed but the inevitable flurry of wisecracks soon turned the explosion of the missile into a mere accident. Although everyone was scared stiff, their pride was soon restored and sprang back up again like the bristles on a thistle.

In my role as the Lady Officer, it was up to me to assure everybody about the complete incompetence of the Red Army: 'For sure, is it even a real army? More like a bunch of hooligans, a rabble, a band of Chinese, which would flee at the first shot from a Russian gun.' 'Well said, Madam – absolutely true!'

Bang! At that very moment another shell exploded over our heads. My heart began to quiver with the wild dance of lively red devils, while the Police Chief, abandoning his superior strategic reasoning till another time, put on a second pair of comfy trousers and hid in the bath, along with all the rest of the household. That's when we first met with our 'downstairs' neighbours.

I came across them on the top rung of the stairs. Poking their heads above the low threshold, women and children looked skyward to the tracery of explosions with bated breath, then towards the bathroom door, behind which the captured goat was anxiously bleating. We understood each other right away. The wife of the worker who had only just been arrested that night moved closer, asked my name in a whisper and then, thinking on, said, 'No, he got away, it said in the paper that he got away, you come in here.'

She juggled her baby into position – it hadn't been able to locate the wide brown nipple on her slender breast – and once again listened out for the rumbling of the artillery. 'What do you reckon – have we pretty much had it already? If the Red Army reaches here today – have we got a chance, or is it already too late?' Not expecting an answer (which she already knew instinctively would be as flat, wooden and dark as the ceiling on the basement) she succumbed to the crescendo of the offensive, from which the whole house was now being shaken.

All around, the rolling thunder grew nearer. It erupted with long, explosive bursts, overwhelming the scanty, but frequent, retaliatory fire. Then, from somewhere on the other side came the din of a new ironclad belch from a powerful steel muzzle. At first, they seemed to strike at random, but increasingly with terrifying precision. Were they meant for us, or somebody else? Alas, we could only make out the distinctive sound made by the barrage, which could not be mistaken.

These explosions weren't taking place directly over Kazan. That meant only one thing – they were aimed at us. For about another hour, the cacophony thundered in the sunny blue sky. Then, it seemed to draw back. Fewer and fewer shells landed on the town and then it quietened down completely. Only in the far distance could you make out the sound of gunfire, neither retreating nor coming any closer, like a rogue wave.

For an hour or two, possibly longer, my new neighbour lay with her head on the threshold, not rousing at all and never once saying a word. Finally, she lifted her face – you could see that the tracks of her tears were coated with dirt and the impact of the assault. Picking up her baby from the steps, she made a beeline for the basement.

Needless to say, just a couple of words in the ear of the Police Chief could have spared these families from the White Terror, but not one of the 'downstairs' families wanted to take advantage of this option. My companion Misha never returned, neither that evening nor the next morning. I found myself alone, with no money and no documents.

The Police Chief initially empathised but then decided that since my 'husband' was a volunteer officer he might have been mobilised when he went to HQ, where he had last been seen. He suggested I go into town to make enquiries. These were familiar streets and familiar houses but nevertheless difficult to recognise. It was as though ten years had passed since our retreat. Everywhere looked completely different. The shops were all open and bustling, dazzlingly-bright cafés were overflowing with officers, high-school students and young women from intelligentsia families wearing Sisters of Mercy scarves. In short, all that ephemeral and tawdry blight which instantly appears on the corpse of a defeated revolution.

On the outskirts, the tram stopped in order to make way for a cart which was loaded down with the naked bodies of executed workers, their limbs sticking out like the branches of a tree. It trundled slowly past a barrier plastered with posters proclaiming: 'All Power to the Constituent Assembly'. Probably, the people who originally thought up this constitutional slogan had never imagined that their mantra would be replicated so often on such cynical, easily comprehensible, revolutionary handbills.

The White Army HQ was located on Gruzinsky Street. Normally, it wasn't that difficult to buy a pass that got you into the office; some head office staff ran past me who had served in the Revolutionary Military Council up to a few days earlier. Milling about at all the doors, there were high-school students, 15 and 16-year-old youngsters. More or less the entire provincial intelligentsia had roused itself, thrown itself into a multitude of bustling activity, getting prepared to carry out government functions, like the voluntary Red Cross, amateur espionage and self-sacrifice on the altar of the Fatherland – all kitted out in stylish riding breeches, with bespoke stirrups and moustaches.

Lord above, how magnificent is the White regime on just the third day of its creation! See how smartly the typists, with their pretty and intelligent feminine looks, clack on their Remington typewriters. The entrance to the command centre was guarded by two well-turned-out soldiers, like the stock-still sentries who used to protect the Royal Box in the old days. Now and then, someone will dart out from these doors in a wide-open military jacket, with a fresh shirt and perfumed moustache. If not a General, then something of the kind, maybe a Colonel or a Captain. How effortlessly, piously and humbly the bureaucratic and military ostentation provides a superficial gloss to this blot on the true enlightenment.

Good grief, my dear *alma mater*, birthplace of Russian state education, it's your dwindling glow which glints on these epaulettes, braids and spurs. In one of my visits to the HQ, I was even able to see in Lieutenant Ivanov's waiting room Mademoiselle Fifi from the White Guards of Kazan, a genuine Professor. She was wearing a loose cloak, with a cape, a modest wide-brimmed floppy hat and underneath it the kind of luxuriant, pure grey hair which has been the fashion for philanthropists, idols of the 'sensitive advanced youth', since the time of Turgenev. In no time, and under her breath, she told the cadet who was listening to her all manner of top secrets about the undesirable elements who she knew to be in hiding in his apartment block.

On the second day, I continued my visits to Gruzinsky Street. I finally managed to find out from a few secretaries and orderlies a list of names of comrades who had been shot, or had escaped. Now it was feasible to contemplate either option – Raskolnikov might not have been shot after all.

The Police Chief, waiting in vain for my missing 'husband', began to show signs of jumpiness. I didn't have a penny, and my downstairs neighbours persistently advised me to get going, before it was too late. Living a life of constant lies, taking part in daily conversations about 'Yids', Communists and the upcoming victories of Orthodox firepower was becoming unbearable.

One morning, I quietly dressed and tucked a crust of bread into my pocket, in which a permit was concealed in the soft part. I'd decided it was time to leave the house and never go back. The worker's wife managed to stuff a three-rouble note in my hand but I was stopped at the gate by the Police Chief.

'So, where are you heading, madam, at such an early hour?'

'To the HQ, they promised to give me some accurate information today.'

'Let me accompany you, I can help, lend you some protection, so to speak.'

'No need to worry – I can manage perfectly well…'

'What worry? No at all, let the old man look after the house.'

No matter how hard I tried to talk him out of it, the Police Chief stood his ground, and my words stuck to his obliging insistence like flies to sticky paper. At the HQ, a secretary appeared out of nowhere and when I passed through the main lobby with him, behind the backs of the clientele and female assistants who were warily eyeing us up, there was the glint of a cold, shiny bayonet.

Lieutenant Ivanov's office was located upstairs, in three small rooms. The first of these, the reception, was stuffed with petitioners, relatives of people who had been arrested for different reasons, and a sentry. While my esteemed escort rushed off to report to Ivanov – that's the very same one who 'in the name of the Revolution' had been right behind the Kazan railway workers, I had time to look around.

And then, in an instant, directly in front of me, I came across a cluster of sailors from my own flotilla. Sailors who, like all the sailors from 1918, imparted the great Russian Revolution with its romantic brilliance. With their strong, open necks, tanned faces and wearing navy caps labelled *Andrey*, *Sevastopol*, and simply, *Red Fleet*.

The bosun looked at me so intently, with eyes I recognised, that I could see right down into his vulnerable, stalwart soul. Wide in the shoulders, with a cross which hung down on a shoelace – not for God, but for happiness. In twenty minutes, he would be up against a wall. For the first few seconds, I'm not sure how many, my pulse was racing. His eyes, which had been appealing to me for help, could no longer see anything – like guns in wet weather they are coated with moisture. Struck with rifle-butts, the sailors are led away. When he reaches the doorway, the bosun turns around. Now his eyes are saying: 'Goodbye'. The room is spinning like mad; from somewhere inside it, the sparkle of water, the brilliance of the sea on a windy day hit by a brief, angry, silvery squall.

A green table, with three officers sitting behind it. No doubt the one on the left is Ivanov. He's got a pale, bald head – so white it looks like a hard-boiled egg. Bright eyes, no eyebrows, white military tunic, spotless white hands on the table. The second one is a Frenchman: I don't recognise his face. There's something peculiarly fastidious about it and resolutely cold. He surveys the room, trying to remember everything exactly, as if he wanted to be able to tell a witty story about it when he got home. The third is there to take minutes of the proceedings. His pen, a permanent fixture, starts with a capital letter at the top of the page, finished off with a sweeping flourish.

'Your surname? Place of birth? Social status?'

To my answers, Ivanov smiles with a broad, almost good-natured grin.

'And you know Raskolnikov?' My face reflects the innocent and carefree demeanour of the Prosecutor.

'Ras-kol-nikov? No, who might that be?'

A long pause

'Lieutenant, Sir, it's impossible to know all of the scoundrels, there's so many of them.'

The Frenchman looks towards us, as though he were watching a farce.

'That's all very well but he's the one we need you to remember.'

I said nothing.

Suddenly, this person – who had just put up with such inventive pauses – beckoned, like a well-fed cat toying with a mouse it doesn't need, towards the foreign officer and displayed the underwear which had been taken from me at the time of my preliminary investigation and strip-search. It was now neatly folded in front of Ivanov's inkwell. Abruptly, this seemingly elegant, nonchalant, witty prosecutor smashed his fist on the table and bellowed in Russian, leaping out of his seat in a hysterical rage.

'I'll show you – you'll sing to me like you sang to your mother – you absolute scoundrel!'

Turning bluntly to the French officer who had committed the *faux pas* of sitting in on the sensitive interrogation, he said,

'Off you go downstairs, I'll call you when I'm ready.'

The Frenchman tip-toed past me, glancing at both myself and his own colleagues and allies with a contemptuous, indifferent, almost smirking look.

Once more, Ivanov spoke quietly, with his previous gentle, ambiguous, deceptive smile.

'Just a moment, we can't do this without an investigator.'

In the room, there were three doors. The one to the right was where Ivanov had left the room; the middle one – the storm door, was covered up with felt, and closed. The third, on the far left, led to the reception. Next to it – a clock.

There are moments in life of fabulous, divine, mad happiness. On this grey morning, which I saw through a window covered with a useless, filigree cross-grille, a miracle happened for me. As soon as Ivanov left the room, the sentry – evidently dumb-founded by the Lieutenant's edgy performance, with his breath-taking transition from ingratiating and sardonic courtesy, to visceral screaming at point-blank range – took the chance to nip out for half an hour, for a smoke.

All that was left in the room were the folds of his overcoat and the heavy wooden butt of his rifle. How long would it take for him to have a cigarette? I managed to run to the boarded-up middle door and tug at it a few times with my remaining strength.

It flew open, missed me and then silently closed again. I found myself on the stairs, managed to remove the bandage that was tied round my face and ran out onto the street. At the window of the General Office, the Police Chief was standing with his back to me, waiting to flatten some flies on the glass. A cabman happened to be going past the HQ in his droshky, in no hurry. He turned around when I jumped into the back seat.

'Where would you like to go?'

I wasn't able to give him an answer. I wanted to, but couldn't. He looked at my semi-transparent attire, at my face, at the HQ, stood up on the driver's seat to his full height and furiously lashed the horse. Rumbling along on the dreadful cobbled pavements of Kazan, through backyards and alleyways, as if in a story-book fable - foaming at the mouth, its tail for once high in the air, the horse all but flew through the gates and into the cab yard.

It turned out that the cabman's son had served in the Red Army and on top of that he was married to the wonderful Avdotya Markovna – fair, lovely and three different widths. She was warm as toast, and gentle like the red sun you see on village headscarves and in fairy tales. She hugged me and I squealed like a piglet on her vast, earth-motherly breasts. She cried too and whispered extra-special, tender words, warm and comforting, like buns still warm from the oven.

Then, she covered my naked shoulders with a shawl and, right there on the porch, listened to the whole story from the beginning, using such foul language to vilify Lieutenant Ivanov that the plump cockerel, scratching at the dung-heap warmed by the sun, clucked with delight.

'Come on, dear – let's have some tea.'

After a couple of hours wrapped in the rose-embroidered shawl, I set off to the Kazan city gates clutching a loaf of bread and three roubles. Too busy inspecting a passing cart, the first control post completely overlooked me; to avoid the next one I crept through the bushes. My peasant companion who agreed to take me to the first village graciously granted me life, on this happiest day of my life. Juddering along at a trot for six miles, he spoke with just the same voice as my 'downstairs' neighbour, and my red-bearded cabman, and Avdotya Markovna, and the entire Russian poor who - in the days of the initial revolutionary turmoil, defeat and retreat - were definitely on our side and for our victory.

They saved people like me, humbly and resolutely, just like they saved thousands of other comrades scattered all over the Russian highways.

'Well, this is where I leave you, miss. This Civil War is all complete nonsense - I see that you eat like a bird, take the road to the village on the left, that's your side down there. To the right over there is a dark cloud: that's the Czechs, the cavalry.'

Running through fields for two miles, I did indeed meet up with our front line. One of the Red Army men, who evidently recognised me from the time we were at Comrade Yudin's headquarters, sat nearby on the ploughed-up ground. Tactfully, pretending that he hadn't noticed how upset I was, and rolling a cigar, he said:

'So, did you find your husband?'

✪ SVIYAZHSK

There will come a time, after many years, when comrades meet up again who had fought together against the Czecho-Slovaks near Kazan in 1918 and afterwards in the Urals, or near Samara and Tsaritsyn. Then, after the first few questions, one of them is sure to ask.

'Do you remember Sviyazhsk?' – and once again they will embrace each other.

So, what exactly is Sviyazhsk?

Today, it's a legend, one of those revolutionary legends which has not yet been recorded by anyone but which is constantly repeated in every part of great Russia. Not a single soldier who ever fought in the Red Army, nor the veterans from the foundation of the Workers and Peasants Army, returning home and reflecting on three years of Civil War, will fail to recall the epic story of Sviyazhsk, the place from which a wave of revolutionary offensives was set in motion which reached into every corner of Russia.

To the east, to the Urals; to the south, to the Caspian Sea; to the west, to Poland. Of course, none of this happened immediately and not all at the same time. It only came about after the Red Army of Sviyazhsk and Kazan crystallised into a military and political force, which – with modifications and improvements – was to become the archetype throughout the Russian Federation of Soviet Socialist Republics.

On 6 August, 1918, numerous hastily-formed regiments were forced to withdraw from Kazan. The best of these, the most politically-conscious element, managed to hang on at Sviyazhsk, dug in and then decided to stay and fight.

At the same time as a crowd of deserters fleeing from Kazan had got themselves as far as Nizhny-Novgorod, the barrier which had been established at Sviyazhsk had already stopped the Czecho-Slovaks, and the general who tried to take the railway bridge across the River Volga by storm was killed during a night-time attack.

Given that the Whites had only just taken Kazan and therefore should have been stronger in terms of both materials and morale, this initial clash with the remnants of the Red Army trying to defend the Volga crossing point, effectively snuffed out the Czecho-Slovakian offensive.

It's very difficult to describe the military significance of Sviyazhsk when we no longer have the material, the maps, the comrades who were part of the 5th Army at that time. Much has already been forgotten, faces and names are recalled as if through a fog. But there's one thing that will never be forgotten: that's the feeling of great responsibility for the protection of the rear-guard action at Sviyazhsk which united all of its defenders, from a member of the Revolutionary Military Council (Revoen) to the very last Red Soldier, who had caught up with his existing regiment somewhere, in a panic, and suddenly turned back, facing Kazan, with his battered rifle in his hands, and with a desperate determination to defend himself to the last.

Everyone understood what the situation was: another step back would open the route via the River Volga to Nizhny Novgorod and then all the way to Moscow. Further retreat would be the beginning of the end, a death sentence for the newly-born Republic of Soviets. Whether this was true from a strategic point of view, I don't know.

It's possible that if the army had rolled back even further, it might have reformed in a similar way on another of the countless black dots which pepper the map, and from there would have carried its banners to victory – but in terms of morale it was the right thing to do. And, since a retreat from the Volga would then have meant a complete collapse, our ability to hold on, to resist, to lean with our backs to the bridge and fight off all sides, gave rise to a feeling of real hope.

The revolutionary sentiment formulated in a difficult situation could be summed up in a few words: retreat would mean the Czech army in Nizhny Novgorod and Moscow.

Sviyazhsk and the bridge do not give up - it was that which made possible the reverse capture of Kazan by the Red Army.

It seems that on the third or fourth day after the fall of Kazan, Trotsky arrived in Sviyazhsk. His train pulled into the small station for a while, the locomotive still puffing.

Then the engine was uncoupled, it went off to have its water tanks refilled – and never came back. A number of its wagons became as immobile as the dirty huts and barracks in which the headquarters of the 5th Army were located. This was a tacit confirmation that nobody would be leaving, there was nowhere to go and it was impossible.

Little by little, what began as the fantastical belief that this small station might become the launchpad for a reverse attack on Kazan began to take shape. During the course of each successive day, this obscure, insignificant railway siding defended its existence against an immeasurably stronger enemy, fortified its position and gradually adjusted to the defiant mood. Reinforcements arrived from somewhere in the rear, from remote villages, first one at a time, then bigger detachments and, finally, more intact military units.

As of now, I see a Sviyazhsk where there is not a single soldier 'under duress'. Everyone who lived here and defended it and everything that was in it was connected by the strongest bonds of voluntary discipline and voluntary participation in a struggle, which at first seemed utterly hopeless.

The people who slept on the floors of the station building, in dirty huts full of broken glass and straw, had practically no real hope of success. Consequently, no one was afraid. No one was interested in how and when it would 'end'. 'Tomorrow' was of no concern. There was going to be a brief, intense, searing passage of time – 'today'. This is what they all lived for, in much the same way as they lived during the time of the harvest.

Morning, daytime, evening, night – every hour is long drawn out, it has to be endured and then outlasted, persevered until the very last second – much in the same way as every slice is sparingly and neatly cut right to the heel of a mature loaf of bread. Every hour seemed precious, not at all like their previous lives – it was barely perceptible now, conjured up as a kind of miracle. Yes, it was a miracle.

A plane flew in and out again, dropping its bombs at the station and railway carriages. Then it drew closer. Evading the sickening barking of its machine guns and the relentless sound of its guns, a man in a tattered overcoat, with a civilian hat and with a pair of boots through which his feet were visible – in other words, one of the defenders of Sviyazhsk, took a watch out of his pocket and, with a smile, thought to himself:

'So, it's half past twelve, or four, or twenty past six. Who cares – I'm still alive. Sviyazhsk is holding on, Trotsky's train is safely under canvas, a lamp has been lit in the window of the political department. Very good. That's me done for the day.'

There were almost no medicines in Sviyazhsk. Heaven knows what the doctors used for bandages. No one was ashamed of this privation and didn't fear it either. Soldiers went to the kitchen for cabbage soup, past stretchers where the wounded and dying lay. Death did not frighten them - it was expected every day, always. Lying in a wet overcoat, with a red blotch on the shirt, with an empty face, no longer a person - it went without saying.

Brotherhood! is a trite, unfortunate word. But sometimes it seems appropriate, in moments of extreme necessity and danger - unselfish, righteous, unique - never again to be experienced in life. The one who has never lived and knows nothing about life, who did not lie at night, louse-ridden and in rags, and did not think that the world is beautiful, and how beautiful!

That the old order has collapsed, that life grapples with bare hands for its irrefutable truth, for the white swans of its resurrection, for something invisible, bigger and better even than this segment of starry sky, visible through a window like velvet but with broken glass - towards the future of all mankind. Once a century they touch and change with living blood. Words like this, such harshly beautiful words - and the smell of the living sweat, the living breath of others sleeping side by side on the floor.

Don't kid yourself, no need for sentimentality – tomorrow will be another day. Comrade G, the Czech Bolshevik, will cook scrambled eggs for the whole company. The Chief of Staff will climb into the rough, frozen shirt that he washed the day before. It's the start of a day when someone will die, knowing in the final seconds that death is, by the way, not the most important thing: the main thing is that Sviyazhsk has still not fallen. On a filthy wall, marked out with a piece of chalk, you can still read the words: 'Proletarians of all countries, Unite!'.

That's the way it went, one rainy day in August after another. The sporadically equipped and inadequately armed barrier did not retreat. The bridge stayed in Bolshevik hands, and from the rear, from somewhere far off, more reinforcements began to arrive.

Our connecting wires hitched themselves to the autumn cobwebs hovering in the wind and gradually some huge, bulky, fragile contraption began to operate next to the remote railway station Sviyazhsk, a miniscule black dot barely visible on the map of Russia, seized in a moment of despair and exodus a month ago by the hand of the Revolution.

This was where all the organizational genius of Trotsky came to the fore. He managed to establish supply lines and push on to Sviyazhsk fresh artillery and several regiments, all essential for a renewed offensive, despite the fact that the railway line had clearly been sabotaged.

At the same time, you need to remember that you were meant to work in 1918, at a time when demobilization was still raging. The appearance of a well-dressed detachment of Red Army soldiers on the streets of Moscow would cause a real sensation. After all, it meant going entirely against the mighty waters of the Revolution, which had dispersed the wreckage of the old Arakcheev[16] school of discipline throughout the entire country. There was still a visceral hatred of anything which smacked of the officer's bullying, regimented barracks and soldiery.

Despite all this, we could still get supplies, newspapers came, boots still arrived, and so did coats. As a matter of fact, the delivery of boots is a serious business – when that happens, it makes for a real, strong headquarters. There is stability, there the army sits tight and does not think to run. It's also a joke - boots!

At the time of Sviyazhsk, there was no such thing as the Order of the Red Banner,[17] otherwise it would need to have been given to hundreds of people. All of them - and that includes some cowards, and people who lost their nerve, ordinary workers and Red Army soldiers - all without exception made impossible, heroic gestures, surmounted their own fears, came out of their shells, joyfully over-spilling their normal capabilities. There was such an atmosphere. I remember a few of the letters we received at that time from the emergency in Moscow. They were about the jubilation of the bourgeoisie, which was getting ready to repeat the memorable days of the Paris Commune.

And this was at the same time as we were fighting on the first and most dangerous front of the Republic, hanging by a thread on a railway line, ablaze, and engulfed by an as-yet unheard of flashpoint, which would last for another three years of hunger, typhoid and war, far from home.

It wasn't just Trotsky who was in Sviyazhsk. Having managed to give the new-born army a backbone of steel, he himself had grown to admire the place. He decided that, whatever happened, he would not interfere with this group of defenders who were able to display a profound, iron-willed composure.

Among them were old party workers, future members of the Revolutionary Military Council of the Republic and of the Revoen Army. A future historian of the Russian Civil War will write about them as marshals of the Great Revolution. Names like Rosengoltz and Gusev, Ivan Nikitich Smirnov,[18] Kobozev, Mezhlauk, another Smirnov and many other comrades, whose names were forgotten. Among the sailors - Raskolnikov and the late Markin.

Almost from the first day, in his railway carriage, Rosengoltz concentrated immediately on the Revolutionary Military Council. Maps were hung up and typewriters clicked and clacked - God knows where they came from. In short, he began to put together a robust, almost geometrically correct organisational machine, with its precise links, unflagging energy and simplicity of operation.

And after all, no-matter which army it might be, on whatever front, the work is not stratified. Now, Rozengoltz was brought there like a queen bee in a sack, put in a ruined hive and immediately began to build uncontrollably, to remove cells, get the telegraph wires buzzing. Despite his greatcoat and the huge pistol under his belt, there was nothing belligerent about his presence and his white, somewhat pasty face. His enormous strength lay not in his military bearing but in his organic ability to revitalise, reconnect, raise to an explosive velocity the flow of bunged-up, congested circulation. Next to Trotsky he was like a dynamo, efficient, unforced, manipulating silent mighty levers, day and night spinning his unbreakable organizational web.

I don't remember exactly what official work Ivan Nikitich Smirnov did at the headquarters of the 5th Army. Whether he was a member of the Revoen Council or simultaneously in charge of the political department. Whatever, beyond all titles and agencies, he personified the revolutionary creed and had the most exemplary moral conviction. He was the communist conscience of Sviyazhsk.

Even among the non-party mass of the soldiers and among the communists who did not know him before, the amazing integrity and decency of Comrade Smirnov was immediately recognised. He would have been barely aware of how afraid they were of him, afraid to show cowardice and weakness in front of him, in front of a man who never shouted at anyone, just by remaining himself - composed and courageous. No one was as respected as Ivan Nikitich. It always felt as though, at the worst moment, he could be relied on to be the strongest and most fearless.

With Trotsky – it was all about the satisfaction of dying in battle, firing to the last bullet, disregarding injuries; with Trotsky – the sublime pathos of the conflict, its words and its gestures, were reminiscent of the best pages of the Great French Revolution.

As for Comrade Smirnov (or so it seemed to us then, as we talked among ourselves in a whisper, lying side-by-side on the floor in cold autumn nights) – well, with Comrade Smirnov, there was a serene composure about him even when he was up against the wall, under the interrogation of the Whites, in a dirty pit of a prison. Yes, that's what they said about him in Sviyazhsk.

Mikhailov[19] arrived a little later, it seems, from Moscow indeed. Direct from the centre. He arrived in his civilian coat, with that light and easily changing expression on his face, which people get when they have been released into the fresh air from prison or from a big city.

Within a few hours, he was completely intoxicated by the madcap atmosphere of Sviyazhsk. In disguise, he went off to carry out reconnaissance deep behind enemy lines among the White forces in Kazan. He came back three days later, tired, with a weather-beaten face and covered with the inevitable head lice. Apart from that, he was still in one piece.

It is interesting to observe how such a deep internal transformation takes place when people who go to the revolutionary front first of all erupt like a thatched roof set on fire at all four corners, and then cool down and set hard-and-fast to become a fireproof, absolutely bright, finished ingot.

The youngest of all was Mezhlauk, Valery Ivanovich. He had a particularly hard time. His brother and wife had stayed in Kazan and were rumoured to have been shot. Subsequently, it turned out that his younger brother really had died, and his wife suffered lots of terrible things. In Sviyazhsk it wasn't customary to complain and talk about their misfortunes. Mezhlauk said nothing about it all, worked, strolled about in his long cavalry coat on the thick autumn mud and everyone drew together around one all-consuming task, one desire: Kazan.

Meanwhile, the Whites concluded that Sviyazhsk, with its strengthened resistance, was growing into something big and dangerous.

The time for occasional attacks and offensives had gone. It needed to be taken at gunpoint, to come at it full strength, with attacks from all sides. But by that time, it was already too late.

Old Slavin, the commander of the 5th Army, was not all that talented, it seemed, but he was definitely well aware of what was expected of him as colonel. He found a decent defensive position, dug in, worked out a defined plan of operation and carried it out with pure Latvian tenacity.

Sviyazhsk emerged, holding its ground like a bull, turning its broad shoulders and lowered head towards Kazan, moving forwards and brandishing its horns, as hard as bayonets.

One sunny autumn morning, the sleek, nimble, high-speed destroyers of the Baltic Fleet arrived at Sviyazhsk. Their appearance caused a sensation. Now the army could feel protected from their side of the river. A series of heavy artillery battles began, which opened up three or four times every day.

Under fire from the batteries hidden on the shore, our flotilla made its way downstream. These sorties were finished off with an unusually daring raid, undertaken on the morning of 9 September by the sailor Markin, one of the founders and first heroes of the Red Fleet. On his clumsy, iron-plated tugboat, he went right down to the Kazan wharves, landed, forced the gunners out of their emplacements with machine-gun fire and removed the locks from several guns.

On another occasion, in the dead of night on 30 August, our ships sailed close to Kazan itself, shelled it, set alight several barges carrying military equipment and food supplies and left without losing a single vessel. By the way, Trotsky joined the commander of the destroyer *Invincible* in the nick of time: just as he was releasing the ropes cleated to the deck of an enemy barge, right below the muzzle of the White Guard guns.

Right in the middle of the return to an offensive mobilisation on Kazan, Commander-in-Chief Joachim Vacietis[20] arrived. Most of the rank-and-file, including myself, had no idea what the summit meeting with him was about – but soon one piece of news did leak out and it was met with great sympathy by everyone.

What we discovered was that our Old Man (which is what Colonel Slavin was called by his comrade-in-arms) had disagreed with the opinion of Vacietis, who insisted on a left-bank operation where the approach is lower and more open. Instead, Slavin wanted to storm Kazan from the right bank, overlooking the city at its highest point, and not from the left as Vacietis had proposed.

But just at the time when the entire 5th Army was spasmodically preparing for the offensive, when its main forces were finally in a position to move forward after a series of difficult battles over several days and all the while withstanding the counter-attacks of the whites - three 'light' units of the Russian White Guards, combining together, decided to put an end to the protracted Sviyazhsk conflict.

Three of the Whites, most experienced commanders - Savinkov,[21] Kappel,[22] and Fortuneov – at the head of a significant detachment, made a desperate raid on the railway station neighbouring Sviyazhsk. The aim of this was to take possession of Sviyazhsk itself and the bridge over the Volga. The raid was conducted brilliantly; after making the deepest detour, the Whites suddenly descended on the station at the major rail junction of Shikhrany, shot it up, took possession of the station buildings, cut connections with the rest of the line, and burned the barrier protecting Shikhrany to the ground.

Not only that: they caught and destroyed all the livestock being kept in the vicinity of the railway junction. I went to witness what had happened at Schikhrany a few hours after the raid. The station bore all the signs of the kind of utterly senseless pogrom violence which marked all the victories of these gentlemen. They were never able to regard themselves as either masters or future inhabitants of territory which they had accidentally and briefly captured.

The carcass of a cow which had been brutally dispatched lay in the yard (it was killed, not humanely slaughtered). The chicken enclosure was full of dead chickens, lying about in ridiculous positions, looking more as you would expect with dead humans. With its well, a small vegetable garden, a water pump and their living quarters, the slaughter had been carried out as if they were people who had been cornered, as if they were Bolsheviks and 'Yids'.

Guts and entrails spilled out all over the place. Animals and things were scattered among the gutted, defiled, gruesome dead bodies.

Next to this brutal, contorted heap in front of what had been people's living quarters, the indescribable, unspeakable death of several railway employees who had been taken by surprise. The Red Army soldiers had not been singled out – which was just as you would expect.

Only in Goya, in his illustrations of the Spanish campaign and guerrilla war do you get a similar harmony of trees bent to one side by the dark wind and the weight of the hanged, combined with roadside dust, blood and stones.

From the Shikhrany station, Savinkov's detachment moved towards Sviyazhsk along the railway line. Our armoured train *Free Russia* was sent out to meet them. It was armed, as far as I can remember, with long-range naval guns. Its commander, however, was not up to the job. Thinking he was surrounded on both sides, he ditched the train and rushed back to the Revolutionary Military Council 'to give a report'.

During his absence *Free Russia* was blown up and set ablaze. The train's black hulk lay, derailed, just off the tracks very close to Sviyazhsk for a long time. After the loss of the armoured train, the corridor to the Volga seemed to be completely wide open. The Whites had now made it to just below Sviyazhsk, not more than 1.5 to 2 miles from the headquarters of the 5th Army. There was panic. Part of the political department, if not the entire political department, rushed to the wharves and the steamboats.

The regiment which had been stationed on the very edge of the River Volga, but further upstream, lost its nerve and took flight, along with its Commander and Commissar. By dawn, its distraught units ended up at the headquarters of the Volga Military Flotilla. All that remained in Sviyazhsk was the headquarters of the 5th Army with its chancellery, and Trotsky's train.

Lev Davidovich (Trotsky) mobilized the entire complement of the train: every scribe, telegraphist, paramedic, or security personnel at the disposal of the chief of staff of the flotilla T. Lepetenko (he was, by the way, one of the most dedicated soldiers of the Revolution, whose biography alone could make a brilliant chapter in this book). In short, everyone who could hold a rifle. The HQ Chancellery block was empty – it no longer had a 'rear'. Everything was directed towards the Whites, close to the station.

From Shikhrany, all the way to the first houses of Sviyazhsk and then closer to Sviyazhsk, even more so, was pitted with bomb craters and littered with the corpses of horses, abandoned weapons and empty shell casings. Having already advanced past the giant obstacle of the armoured train - still smouldering, smelling of smoke and molten metal - the offensive came to a halt, menaced at the final threshold, receded, then once again threw itself at the reserve army, hastily mobilised to the barricade at Sviyazhsk. For several hours, heaps of dead bodies were piling up on top of each other.

The Whites decided that what was ahead of them now must be fresh forces, well-organized, the presence of which their counter-intelligence must have known nothing about.

Exhausted after their 48-hour raid, the soldiers misconstrued what they were up against – actually a handful of random fighters, behind whom there is nothing, apart from Trotsky and Slavin. They were both bent over a map in a smoke-filled, restless room at HQ, in the middle of empty, abandoned Sviyazhsk, on the streets of which bullets were whistling.

On that night, like all others, Lev Davidovich's train stood on the tracks without a locomotive, and no part of the 5th Army, which forged far ahead and was got ready to storm Kazan, was left undisturbed that night. All of it was sent to the front to cover the almost defenceless Sviyazhsk. The army and flotilla learned all about the night attack after it was all over. By then, the whites were already leaving, convinced that there must be almost a whole division in front of them.

The next day, twenty-seven deserters who had escaped on steam-boats at the most important moment were tried and shot. Among them were several Communists. A lot was said about the execution of these twenty-seven afterwards. This was especially the case away from the frontline, where they do not know on just how thin a thread our defence of the road to Moscow was hanging, and how crucial that was for the final effort of the offensive on Kazan.

To begin with, the whole army was saying that the Communists were cowards, that the law didn't apply to them, that they could desert with impunity whereas an ordinary Red Army soldier would have been shot like a dog.

If it hadn't been for the exceptional courage of Trotsky, the commander and other members of the Revolutionary Military Council, the prestige of the communists working in the army would have been destroyed and lost for a long time.

No suitable words can be found to persuade an army that suffers all sorts of hardships for six weeks, fights with its bare hands and without bandages, that cowardice is not cowardice and that there are some 'mitigating circumstances' for it.

It was argued that among those who were executed were good comrades. Among them were those whose guilt should be set against their previous merits - years of imprisonment and exile. That's all absolutely true. No one claims that their death is one of those moral principles of the old military ethic - which under the beat of a drum meant measure for measure and tooth for a tooth. Of course, Sviyazhsk is a tragedy.

But anyone who lived through the same experience as the Red Army, conceived, forged and hardened in the battles near Kazan, can confirm that it would never have crystallised its iron spirit, there would never have been this adhesion in the eyes of the entire army, which was preparing to make such a great and bloody sacrifice for the Revolution, party and the mass of the soldiers, between the rank-and-file and the command staff.

In the eyes of the entire army, which was preparing to make such a great and bloody sacrifice for the Revolution, this would not have been possible if the Party itself, on the eve of the Kazan assault – in which hundreds of soldiers would inevitably be killed - had not made clear that it had the courage to apply the hard-hitting laws of fraternal discipline in the Soviet Republic to its own members.

After the twenty-seven had been executed, it created a breach, which the celebrated attackers still managed to overcome through the self-awareness and the unity of the 5th Army. The execution of Communists as well as commanders and ordinary soldiers for cowardice and dishonour in battle, forced the worst and most backward section of the army, which was itself prone to desertion (and such a thing did exist) to level up to the rest of the army who went into battle consciously and without needing to be pushed.

The fate of Kazan was decided in these days. Not just the future of Kazan, but the future of the entire White intervention.

The Red Army found itself, re-equipped and strengthened in the long weeks of defence and offensive.

In the conditions of constant danger and the highest moral stress, it worked out and devised its own set of rules, its discipline, its heroic new commands. Here for the first time, the panic and fear induced by the more advanced enemy technique and equipment began to clear. Now the army learned how to bypass any artillery and, unwittingly, based on simple self-defence, learned to develop those new military tactics, those specific methods, which are already being studied by top academies as techniques of Civil War. It was very important in days such as these that there was a man like Trotsky in Sviyazhsk.

No-matter who he might have been, or whatever his name, the creator of the Red Army and the future chairman of the Revolutionary Military Council of the Republic had to be in Sviyazhsk, had to study at first hand the experience of these fighting weeks and use all his willpower and all his organisational genius in its defence. A defence which was forged under fire from a resurgent White army.

And then, in a revolutionary war, there is another force, another component, without which there is no victory. That is the mighty romance of the revolution, without which people would not throw themselves at the barricades and adapt to the unyielding regulations of the military. My own short, easy steps, were acquired on political demonstrations, which do not come about just by resourcefulness and independence, but which are created, perhaps, by many years of party work in the underground.

To win in 1918, it was necessary to take all the fire of the Revolution, all its destructive fervour and disguise it with the vulgar, ugly, old as the world, disposition of the army.

Until now, history has always resolved this question impressively, but played it for theatrical effect. You send an actor on to the stage in a 'three-cornered hat and grey hiking coat', and he, or another general on a white horse, slash republican uniforms, banners and slogans from living revolutionary flesh. In its military composition, as well as in many other things, the Russian Revolution went its own way. Revolt and war merged into one.

The army and the party merged, fused permanently, and recorded all the distinct slogans of class struggle and the unity of their goals on their regimental banners. In the days of Sviyazhsk, all this was not yet formalized, but the air was charged with it, looking for its expression. The Workers and Peasants Army somehow had to have an impact, to make its presence felt, to have its concept – but, at this stage, nobody knew definitely what that was. There was nothing in writing, no kind of dogmatic programme, by means of which this gigantic body was to grow and develop.

In the party and in the masses, there was just a presentiment, a form of creative guesswork of what this military-revolutionary organization - of a type which had never been seen before - might look like. Every day of battle provided some new example. Trotsky's merit was that he instantly sensed the slightest shift in movement of the masses, who already carried the imprint of this unique organisational formulation, which was being fumbled towards.

Thanks to the lessons learned at a beleaguered Sviyazhsk, he was able to identify and then entrench all of those minor advances which precipitated the simplification, acceleration and reconfiguration of combat operations. And not only in a narrow, technical sense. No, every new and successful category of *Specialist* and *Commissioner* – that is, the person who gives the orders and the one who executes the order and has responsibility for it – had been put to the test through experience, was clearly formulated and then immediately issued as a command, a bulletin, a directive. In this way, the living revolutionary experience was not wasted, not forgotten, not distorted.

Not being average became the norm. It became obligatory for all. That meant adopting the best, most brilliant tactics conceived by the masses in the most intense and most creative moment of the struggle. Whether it be a major or minor issue, no-matter how difficult or confusing – such as the division of labour between the members of the Revolutionary Military Council - or the quick, friendly gesture, with which a red commander and his soldiers are expected to greet each other, on an equal footing, even though both are running somewhere on business - all this had to be witnessed first-hand, memorized, and then re-introduced into the masses for general use. And when it didn't work, it creaked or was confusing – the problem needed to be assessed, addressed or coaxed along, like a midwife would do during a difficult labour.

It's possible to be an excellent advocate, to provide a new army with a rational, infallible, even sculptural composition but nevertheless freeze its spirit, allow it to evaporate, not know how to go beyond the bounds of legalistic formulations. To prevent this from happening, you need to be a great revolutionary. You need to have a creative intuition, a tip-top internal antenna, without which it is impossible to connect with the masses.

When all's said and done, it is this revolutionary instinct that permits the final endorsement. This is what distinguishes the new way of doing things from all that is deep-rooted, half-baked, counter-revolutionary. Trotsky breaks all the rules of a deceitful formal justice in the name of the higher, proletarian variety. He does not allow versatile regulations to ossify, to be detached from life, to weigh down on the shoulders of the Red Army with the petty, annoying, and unnecessary. Trotsky had this intuitive sensitivity.

It was never the case that he allowed being a soldier, a warlord, or a commander to overshadow the revolutionary in him. And when he came down on the deserters with his merciless, terrible pronouncement, they were afraid of him as one of their own, as a great rebel, for treason not to the military, but to the all-proletarian, revolutionary cause.

Trotsky was not capable of being a coward – otherwise he would have been crushed by the contempt of this exceptional army. It would never forgive the weakness of the twenty-seven deserters, whose brotherly blood splattered its first victory.

A few days before the occupation of Kazan by our troops, Lev Davidovich (Trotsky) left Sviyazhsk; he was summoned to Moscow by the news of an assassination attempt on Comrade Lenin. But neither Savinkov's raid on Sviyazhsk, organized by the Socialist Revolutionaries with great skill, nor the attempt to kill Ilyich – made by the same party and almost simultaneously with the Savinkov raid – could not stop the Red Army, and the ninth wave of the offensive fell upon Kazan.

In the dead of night, from 9 September to 10 September, troops were loaded onto ships and by 5.30, at dawn, hulking great multi-storey ships guarded by destroyers descended upon the Kazan marinas.

In the lunar twilight it was so strange to sail past a dilapidated mill with a green roof, behind which a battery of Whites usually hid, past the burnt-out *Dolphin*, scorched and abandoned on the deserted shore, past all the familiar bends, outcrops, shallows and backwaters, over which for so many weeks from morning to night death had run amok and where smoke billowed amid golden flashes of gunfire.

We proceed, with lights out, in absolute silence, across the black, cold, smoothly flowing waters of the River Volga. Behind the stern, a little foam on a muffled, murmuring backwash, carelessly running down to the Caspian, washing it all away and remembering nothing. The choppy waters here, in which now even this giant ship cannot be heard, were still being bombarded and furiously ploughed up with cannon-fire as recently as yesterday. This is where a night bird has now returned. Its wings are silently brushing the surface of the water and the vapour rising from the cold.

This is where so many commands had been issued, and where, amid the fire and smoke, sleek destroyers, peppered with shrapnel, trembled from the dormant energy of their engines and from the minute-by-minute eruption of their twin guns, like iron hiccups. They fired, escaped the hail of returning fire, wiped blood from the deck.

Now, silently, the Volga flows on, just as it flowed a thousand years ago, and as it will flow in centuries to come. We reach the wharves without a single shot being fired. It's getting light. In the pink-grey twilight, hunched, black, burnt ghosts began to appear. Crane hoists, the charred beams of burned-out buildings, split telegraph poles – all this is something endlessly suffered, a lost sensitivity, similar to trees with contorted, bare branches. A dead kingdom, quilted with the cold roses of a northern dawn. And cannons at the ready, with raised muzzles, appearing at dusk like defeated figures, frozen in mute despair, with their heads raised upwards and braced by cold hands, wet from the dew.

Fog, people tremble with cold and nervous tension, smells of machine oil, resin from ropes. The blue collar of the gunner rotates, like his gun on its pedestal, in astonishment – taking in the desolate, dumb, dead silence of the slumbering shore.

It's a victory.

✪ FROM KAZAN TO SARAPUL

The night bells, which ring out the hours on the deck of the destroyer, are remarkably similar to the chimes of the Peter and Paul fortress. But, instead of the Neva, majestically at rest, instead of muted granite and golden spires, their distinctive sound descends on uninhabited shores, the clear, unpredictable waters of the River Kama, islands of lost villages.

It's dark on the bridge. The moon barely illuminates the sleek, elongated and streamlined super-structure of the battleships. Sparks flare from their funnels, milky smoke swirls towards the water like a white mane, and the ships themselves, with their proudly raised prows, appear in the midst of these wild expanses not as the last word in progress, but more like menacing and stealthy leviathans.

In the sparse lighting, individual faces are pale but as distinctly visible as during the day. Silent and somewhat distinct poses. The movements of the commandant, who is a cultured individual, with a debonair demeanour, who whips the heavy tarpaulin from a gun with a single flourish, just as in a ballet the veil would be plucked from a bewitched and terrifying head.

The hands of the signaller whirl about, with his red flags eloquently and concisely marking out a ceremonial dance of instructions and responses on the night wind.

High overhead, above the mast and the bridge, above the pent-up nervous tension of a ship preparing for battle, above the glow from its red-hot furnace, concealing its smoke and heat in the depths of its hold, and amid its faintly shimmering rays, a green morning star arises.

It's a while since we sailed from and left behind the turn of the river where we had our advanced post. On the same shore was another boat and the commander of the Smolensk regiment, Ovchinnikov. Always calm, unhurried, steadfast, precise and a man of few words – he was part of what became the glorious 28th Azinsky Division[23] and went with it into battle across the whole of Russia, from the cold River Kama to the blistering hot winds of Baku.

Somewhere to the right, an elusive light flashes. It could be the Whites, or it could be one of Kozhevnikov's partisan detachments, on patrol deep within enemy lines. Now and again they reappear completely unexpectedly, climbing out to meet us at low water level from the impenetrably thick shrubbery which entangles the steep rocky shoreline of the River Kama.

At the first rays of dawn the beauty of these shores is extraordinary. The Kama near Sarapul is wide and deep, flowing among the yellow clay cliffs, splitting between the islands, and carrying on its oily-smooth surface the reflection of fir trees. As such, it is free and so calm. The silent destroyers do not disturb the captivating peace of the river.

Hundreds of swans are dotted along its banks, their white wings ventilated by the late October sun. A flurry of ducks creates a momentary shadow as it rushes to land on the water. Far above the white church on the shore, an eagle circles and soars. Even though the meadow on the opposite shore is occupied by the enemy, not a single shot is heard from its low-lying ground cover. Obviously, we were not expected here - and they haven't had time to prepare for our arrival.

A pale-faced mechanic, covered in soot, appears half-way from a hatch, up to the waist. Wiping the muck and sweat away from his face, he inhales the sharp morning air with pleasure. In one night, it's become autumnal and feels more northernly.

The pilot is on the bridge. He's dishevelled and sturdy. Looking like Leshy,[24] the wood demon, with his grey hair and sheepskin coat, he predicts an early frost.

'You can smell the snow. There's snow in the air.'

Then, without a sound, he goes back to seeking out a passage for our ships amid the treacherous ripples of shoals, mist and boulders. During the course of one night, we have covered more than a hundred miles. In the distance, the fretwork of a railway bridge comes into view and the white peaks of Sarapul. The crew relaxes, freshens up near the crane and teases the two black puppies which have grown up with great love and attention on continuous voyages, in amongst the cannonballs.

There's a shout from the look-out:

'People on the left bank,' followed by bated breath.

But those on the shore have already seen us - red cloths are being waved joyfully in the breeze. Further along the shore, on the bridge, and beyond the sandy embankment red flags are fluttering. Small figures of marines in grey coats rush along the bank, waving, shouting and casting exuberant greetings towards the iron decks of the destroyers. We pass under the bridge, turn to the left, and behind the last ship, which is following in the wake of the slender column, a gunfight has already broken out. It's the Whites firing at the guards who had come down from the bridge to watch the passage of our flotilla.

The embankment of Sarapul can clearly be seen in our binoculars. It's occupied by the Azin division. Sarapul, surrounded on all sides by the Whites, but finally - thanks to the arrival of our flotilla - now connected to the armies further downstream.

We need to get closer. People are perched on the roofs of shops, along the railings, on the road – among them are Red Army soldiers, nouveau-riche with their handkerchiefs and beards, all of them, astonished and over-joyed that we are their own, friendly forces. The orchestra on the hill blares out the Marseillaise. The drummer, too interested in the ships, misses his beat in the tune, the trumpet player rushes far ahead of the irate conductor, joyfully playing thunderous overtures and not stopping at anything, like a horse that has overthrown its rider. The ship's ropes have already been cleated up, the disembarking ramp has alighted smoothly on the wharf, the sailors have poured ashore and the conversations begin:

'How on earth did you manage to break through? Did they hit any of the ships?'

'They hammered us, old fella, and drove us into the White River.[25]

'Liar.'

'I'm not lying.'

A woman sneaks through the crowd, still very young and all in tears.

'A sailor's wife,' the people gathered round are saying. And new lamentations begin. The cry of a mother and a wife, a piercing monotonous wail:

'Mine was taken away on a barge. They stole him and took him onto the barge. He was a sailor, just like you.'

A handkerchief is passed from one sailor to another, blinded by tears. He pats the sleeves of a dead sailor's rough navy tunic; this is his last memory. Yes, it's a cruel thing is war, Civil War is even worse. How many conscious, deliberate, cold atrocities have retreating enemies managed to commit?

Chistopol, Elabuga, Chelny and Sarapul - all these small towns are dripping with blood. Ordinary villages are inscribed in the history of the Revolution with burning memories. In one place, the wives and children of the Red Army soldiers were flung into the Kama and even babes-in-arms were not spared. In another – the dried-up puddles on the road are still red with blood to this day, and around them an exquisite blush of

*The Vanya-Communist (Ваня – Коммунист) *was a paddle-steamer and tugboat converted to a gunboat with the addition of front and rear cannons on the deck.*

autumn maples seems to commemorate what happened there.

The wives and children of those killed here don't flee the country. They don't write memoirs later on about the burning of the old estate with its Rembrandts and its library or about the furious rampages of the Czechs. No one will ever know, no one will ever sound off to an over-sensitive Europe about the thousands of soldiers shot on the high bank of the River Kama and buried by the current in the muddy shallows which inundate the uninhabited shoreline.

Was there ever a day - I ask all of you who served onboard the *Dependable*, the *Steadfast* and the *Ardent*, on the *Seryozha'* battery emplacement, on the *Vanya-Communist* gunboat[26] or on any of our clumsy, ironclad bathtubs – was there ever a single day when you didn't see a soldier go over the side of the boat in his greatcoat, with the tufts of cropped hair that you get after a bout of typhus evident on the back of his head, his hand bobbing up and down in the water and then sinking to the bottom?

Torpedo-boat Соколъ (Sokol – or Falcon) later renamed Прытку (Priitky – or Nimble) *of the type used by the Bolsheviks on the River Volga. Built for the Russian Imperial Navy at Yarrows Shipbuilders on the River Clyde.*

Was there ever even one place along the River Kama, where no one would howl in pain when you arrived, regardless of where they might be on the shore, either among those who are overjoyed or those beside themselves with worry. Would there not have been, among those who were so inept at tackling your mooring ropes (because they are workers, not sailors), a dozen orphaned women and the dirty, weak and hungry children of workers. Remember this wailing, which could not be drowned out even by the clanking of the anchor chain, even by the furious thumping of the heart, or even when the voice of the executive committee man, raw from the effort, shouted from a distance of half a mile away: 'Samara has been taken by the Reds...'

Meanwhile, the first woman is approached by a second woman, very small and old. She has the same traces of grief on her face.

'Don't cry, tell me straight.'

So, the mother tells her everything, but her words are lost in weeping and wailing, none of it could be comprehended. And here's the thing: while they were retreating, the Whites loaded six hundred of our people on a barge and took them away. Nobody knows where it went – possibly to Ufa, and maybe to the factory at Votkinsk.

An hour later, the ear-piercing sound of a siren gathers the dispersed sailors together on the wharf-side. The commander gives a new order: the flotilla will go up the river in search of the barge with all the prisoners. And, to reinforce his command, makes a point of repeating, especially clearly: 'Six hundred people, comrades'.

They hadn't been expecting us: trenches, barbed-wire fences, pickets on guard - all of this is clearly visible from the river. It is all laid out on a plate. Slowly gliding along the shore, the torpedo-boats choose a convenient place, and the commanders search for a target. From the officers' mess, the hatch is opened to the powder cellar. From there, shells are quickly lifted to the deck. The command is issued:

'Open fire!'

A fiery blast bursts out of the muzzle, an empty casing falls with a slight metallic clang, and 10-15 seconds afterwards a plume of ash-grey and black smoke explodes in the fleeing ranks of the enemy. The gunner in charge re-adjusts his sights.

'Two more, one to the left. Fire!'

Ourselves and the *Ardent* both opened fire and the stern gun on the *Resilient* lights up the church. Utilising the general confusion, we make it to Gallian by nightfall (about 35 miles upriver from Sarapul).

Another ten miles further and we've reached our target. Our red flags are lowered, it was decided to take the enemy by surprise, posing as a White Guard flotilla led by Admiral Stark. They are still waiting for him impatiently themselves, to assist in the defence of Ivezhsk. Because of the small islands and the bends in the River Kama, our ships appeared out of the blue in front of the marinas at Gallian. We passed the village located on the mountain, and beyond that make a turn and then swing around. It is a manoeuvre which is very difficult to do in such a narrow and confined space.

'You can't open fire without orders,' the signaller indicated from one torpedo-boat to another.

The situation is as follows: a heavy 6-inch gun can be clearly seen, situated in among 20–30 saplings on the shore, near the church. A bit further back, on a hillock, lots of inquisitive peasants have assembled, among them a handful of armed soldiers. There's a second gun on the bell tower, it could be a machine gun. Under the left bank is a barge with a troop of White Guards. The white tents of their camp are discernible through the bushes, with the smoke from their outdoor kitchen filtering through. Some soldiers who are relaxing on the shore follow the manoeuvres being made by the destroyers with interest. In the middle of the river, watched over by a guard, a veritable floating grave, silent and motionless.

A voice on the loud-hailer from the *Steadfast*, conveys the order for action to other vessels in an undertone. The *Ardent* approaches the barge and, without giving anything away, makes its presence known to the precious living cargo. The *Steadfast* swivels its guns to take aim at the 6-inch cannon, with a view to destroying it at point-blank range on the first sign of movement from the enemy, but at the same time keeping a close watch on the infantry.

But how are we going to remove the barge from its anchor? How will we manage to pull it out from the narrow confines formed by the riverbank, small islands and shallows? Fortunately for us, the enemy tug *Dawn* stays puffing at the pier-side. One of our officers, in a shiny navy cap, issues their captain with this uninviting order:

'In the name of the commander of the flotilla, Admiral Stark orders you to approach the barge with the prisoners, take it in tow and follow us across the White River to Ufa.'

Accustomed to following orders from the Whites, the captain of the *Dawn*, immediately executes the order. He approaches the barge to take it in tow. These minutes drag out infinitely slowly, while the sluggish tugboat, with its port and starboard paddle-wheels noisily slapping the water, pulls alongside the barge, attaches the ropes, belches smoke and gets up steam. Our command is frozen to the spot. Peoples' faces had turned terribly pale. They wanted to believe but cannot trust this fairy tale in reality, this doomed barge, so close and yet so far away. They whisper to each other, holding their breath.

'Well, is it moving or not?' 'No, it's not moving.'

But the tugboat, *Dawn*, alarmed by the captain's blunt command does exactly as it is told. There's no movement on the barge. The guards on sentry duty, and their commander, down their rifles and help to lift the anchor. Little by little, the hefty bulk of the barge shifts its equilibrium, its prow turns hard around with great difficulty, the tight ropes gradually weaken and once more the tug pulls away trailing its reluctant companion. No doubt, the presence of the *Steadfast* helps to mollify the confused jailers.

'In the name of the commander, I order you to remain completely calm, we will go ahead and escort you in a convoy.'

'We don't have enough firewood', the *Dawn* objects.

'Never mind, we'll give you some more on the way,' replies the Red Fleet commander. Taking their time, so as not to arouse suspicions of the White Guards watching from the shore, the destroyers begin to head for Sarapul.

Meanwhile, in the hold of the barge, the alarm bells have already started to ring, 'Why are we being moved? Where are we being taken…and who by?' One of the prisoners, a sailor, forces his way into the stern along the disgusting, filthy floor. He makes a hole in the thick decking with a penknife at the only point where a piece of sky and the river can be seen. For a long time, and very carefully, he watches the mysterious ships and their silent command. The faces all around him seem to merge with a single contorted expression, impassive and immobile, trying to work out if they can see a ray of hope on his face, or a something new to worry about.

'Yes, after all they all look the same – they're long and grey.'

'Are they White Guards or not? Look closely, hurry up.'

'No, I don't think so.'

'What do you mean don't think so, dickhead?'

The sailor falls off his stool.

'Their ships aren't clad with that kind of iron, they're ours, and the sailors on them are from the Baltic Fleet.'

But the wretches who have spent three weeks below decks in this revolting dungeon, sleeping and eating amongst their own excrement, naked and wrapped in a single blanket, don't dare believe it. They were the same when they got to Sarapul, and the people who had come to greet them shouted and cried on the pier-side. Even when the sailors who had by now arrested the White Guards called on them to come up from their vestibule, but were reluctant to go down into it themselves, they still responded with curses and groans.

Not one of the prisoners believed in the possibility of salvation. It was only yesterday, after all, when the guards were bartering a crust of bread and a kettle for the remaining shirts on their backs. Yesterday at dawn, the torn bodies of three Krasnoperov brothers and twenty-seven other people were lifted up from the prison cell on seven bayonets. It's already been twenty-four hours since anybody threw a piece of bread down through the hole in the ceiling, a quarter of a slice for each person. That was the only food that had staved off the hunger for three weeks.

Since they hadn't been fed, it made no sense to waste even the leftovers on the doomed captives. Whether it would be that night or in the next grey, anaemic morning hour the end would come for them all. Exactly what or when that will be is still unknown, but it weighs upon all of them. And then, all of a sudden, we arrive, open a blue and silver hole in the night sky and call everyone upstairs in strange, terribly anxious voices – using that forbidden, banished name - 'Comrade'. Isn't that treason. Isn't this just another trap, a new deception?

Nonetheless, one by one, crawling on hands and knees with tears in their eyes, they are all raised from the dead. What will be waiting for them on deck? Some Chinese prisoners, who don't have any family in this cold country, fell at the feet of a sailor and gabbled some exclamations in a language we didn't understand, giving thanks and expressing devotion to the comradeship of people prepared to die for each other.

Next morning, the city and the troops met the prisoners. The prison barge is brought to the shore, discarding its resemblance to Stenka Razin[27] – a huge ironclad barge, armed with long-range guns. Through the living wall of sailors, all four hundred and thirty-two of the pale, unkempt and stumbling captives lurch onto the shore. Strung out in a line and dressed up in makeshift sacking, with boots and hats made from twisted straw, this procession of survivors from another world must have appeared a fantastic sight. And in the crowd, still shocked by this spectacle, a wonderful sense of humour already surfaces:

'Who's the one who dressed you up like that, Comrades?'
'Look, look, this is what they do in the Constituent
Assembly – everyone to the forest with a rope around the
neck!'

'Don't step on my boots – look, the toes are poking out!'

And sticks out a leg wrapped in filthy rags'.

As they approached the shore, with voices lying on rotten straw, they began to sing the Marseilles. The singing does not stop until they get to the square. Here, a representative from the prisoners welcomes the sailors of the Volga Flotilla, its commander and the power of the Soviets. Raskolnikov is carried aloft into the dining room, where hot food and tea are prepared. Indescribable faces, words, tears, when a whole family, which has found a father, a brother or a son, sits beside him while he dines and talks about being taken prisoner. Then, saying goodbye, they go to meet their sailor-comrades, to thank them for their deliverance.

Among the crowd of sailors and soldiers, you can make out the caps of the few officers who made the entire three-month journey from Kazan to Sarapul. I think it must have been a long time since they've been met with such boundless respect, with such brotherly love, as they are today. And if there is a miraculous unity between the intelligentsia and the masses in their spirit, in their exploits and in their sacrifice, it was born when the mother of the workers, their wives and their children blessed sailors and officers for getting rid of the execution and torment of their children.

☉ MARKIN

Every morning, the bosun of our flagship *Ebb Tide* looks pleased. With a smile, he reports a drop in temperature in the River Kama. Today the thermometer stopped at 0.5 degrees, zero in the air. Lumps of ice drift downstream, the water has become heavy and slow, there is a constant fog smoking over the surface, a sure harbinger of frost. The crews of the ships, who have survived all the difficult campaigns, from Kazan to Sarapul, are preparing for the winter. They're delighted, looking forward to the rest. Another day or two, and the flotilla will leave the River Kama for good, until next spring.

It's only now, when the time for their obligatory retreat draws near, that everyone suddenly begins to recognise how unforgettable these shores have become and how much they are appreciated - every turn in the river, every wild spruce clinging to the steep cliffs, all recaptured from the enemy.

How many difficult hours of waiting there have been, how many hopes and fears - not for myself, of course, but for the great year of 1918, whose fate often seems to depend so much simply on the accuracy of the shot, on the courage of the scout! How many joyful hours of victory have taken place here on the Kama! Soon the ice will stiffen its unforgiving waters, churned up by shells unleashed from raised decks by both our best comrades and our fiercest enemies.

Who knows, who we will be fighting against next year and which waters that will be in. Who will the comrades be, the next ones to clamber on the armoured bridges of the ships, which have become so familiar and admired by each of us?

With its paddle-wheels thumping and its signal lantern swaying high in the darkness up on the mast, the troop supply-ship heads off towards Nizhny Novgorod. The remaining vessels see off their departing comrade with intermittent blasts from their sirens. This goes on for a long time: each of them sounds as familiar as the voice of a friend. Here goes the rasping wail of *Roshal*,[28] here the abrupt, piercing whistle of *Volodarsky*,[29] here *Comrade Markin*[30] with its deep, deafening foghorn.

This farewell salute made by the sailors is a connection with the most difficult memories. It is resorted to by vessels when they face extreme danger. That's how the unfortunate *Vanya-Communist* called for assistance when it was hit by an enemy shell and set ablaze amid the icy waters of the river, enveloped by explosions, with a broken-down steering wheel and a faulty telegraph. Its siren screamed continuously for a long time.

Increasingly, great plumes of water erupted all around and black dots began to appear on the surface of the river - people who were frantically trying to make it to the shore. Charred debris of wood, some buckets and stools were floating away in the current, and still it didn't stop - shrouded in steam, scorched by fire, in pain, the terrible siren of death.

This calamity was baffling and unexpected. Just the day before, our fleet had won a significant victory over the White Guard flotilla. After a two-day battle near the village of Bitki, the Whites had been forced upstream, and our ships had broken into the rear of their fleet, located on both shores. The pursuit continued for a whole day, and it was only on the morning of the third day that we took anchor on a wonderful stretch of the River Kama, bathed in colours of blue, turquoise and amber, under a clear November sun.

It was decided to stop for a while, to wait for the arrival of the paratroopers. The scouts had brought us alarming news about the strong coastal fortifications in the village of Pyani Bor (the Drunken Forest) that could not be taken from the river without the support of our infantry. On top of that, our stock of ammunition was completely depleted – we only had 18-50 shells left on all the ships and barges. While we were waiting for the infantry, which was always very late, a few motor boats went to do a recce. The sailors set off with pleasure to carry out their search at such a high speed that their elusive outline was barely visible in the sprays of foam, which the Whites opened up on with a completely useless hurricane of gun-fire.

Within the high pillars of water created by the shells, fiery arcs flared. Every minute, the river heaved with foaming white and rainbow fountains which then melted away. A flock of frightened swans rose up from the shallows, a seaplane flew past and buzzed them until the air was filled with the screeching of swans, the agitation of their white wings and the droning of the propeller.

And Markin couldn't stand it. Markin, who commanded the best of the gunboats, *Vanya-Communist*, was accustomed to danger. He'd been in love with it since he was a boy, was unable to stand by and watch the skirmish this morning from the sidelines. He was tantalised by and drawn to the high sandy cliff of Pyani Bor and lurking at its edge, this mysterious emplacement, hidden somewhere on the shore, patiently waiting.

How they lifted anchor, how they crept along the forbidden shore, how they managed to move away from their position – no one could remember well. But suddenly not far away, practically right in front of him, Markin spotted camouflage and behind it the muzzle of a gun pointed directly at him.

One ship cannot take on a coastal battery – but this morning after a victory which had been so intoxicating and so reckless, the *Vanya-Communist* did not back down, did not retreat, but defiantly approached the shore, firing its machine-guns at the soldiers manning the big gun. We like to sing to the glory of the madness of the brave. But this time Markin's death was a foregone conclusion.

The destroyer *Ardent* came to the aid of the *Vanya-Communist* which had gone far ahead. It's wrong to believe in premonitions, but what an agonising dread was being felt by all those then on the bridge of the *Ardent*. This is not fear – no one was exposed to that hcinous syndrome – but a unique, pickling sensation which I personally also experienced when our destroyer, not suspecting anything untoward, approached the *Vanya-Communist*.

The brief conversation from ship to ship was the last one Markin ever had. The fleet commander asked on a megaphone:

'Markin, who are you firing at?'

'We're firing at the emplacement.'

'What emplacement?'

'There behind the screen, you see, the muzzle is shining.'

Immediately he was instructed to withdraw.

But it was too late. As soon as the destroyer's engines began to move into reverse, as soon as the *Vanya-Communist* followed on – the Whites on the shore, feeling that the prey was slipping away from them, opened rapid fire. The shells rained down in a hail. Behind the stern, on either side, in front of the prow – all around. They whizzed across the bridge with a 'sucking' howl, like bowling balls rotating and tearing through the air. Only a few minutes later, the *Vanya-Communist* was shrouded in a cloud of steam, out of which dancing, golden tongues leapt out, and she lurched from one riverbank to the other with a broken steering wheel. It was then that the siren began to scream for help.

Despite the heavy artillery fire, we made our way back to the stricken gunboat, hoping to take her in tow and put out the fire.

But there are conditions under which even the highest courage is ineffective: the first shell which landed on the *Vanya-Communist* hit the steering wheel and damaged the telegraph. The ship was unsailable. It spun on the spot, and the destroyer – which took a great risk in approaching it – was unable to take the dying ship in tow.

The *Ardent*, having made a steep turn, had to get out of there.

How the Whites managed to miss us is simply not clear. They shot at point-blank range. Only the astonishing speed of the destroyer and the firepower of its guns allowed us to escape the trap. And, strangely, two large seagulls, not afraid of the gunfire, flew to and fro in front of the prow for a long time, disappearing momentarily when the shell-bursts hit the water.

Among those who survived was Comrade Poplevin, Markin's assistant. He was a reticent man, extraordinarily modest and courageous, one of the best in the flotilla. But he retained a bluish paleness on his face for a long time – it left the traces of death especially clearly when the autumn sky shone cloudless and the waves splashed imperturbably on the golden shores of the Kama.

He made amends for his friend and for the death of his ship. At night, when even the most indefatigable were tired, Poplevin silently climbed up to the bridge and looked out all alone under a dark starry sky. He listened out, sensing the slightest movement of the night. He never tired and his unbreakable desire for revenge never weakened.

He waited for Markin all night but Markin did not return. He was dejected standing at the wheel like a silent helmsman, with the gunners at their guns, and look-outs at their viewing screens, which suddenly seemed to have clouded over from unshed tears.

Markin died and took with him his fiery temperament, his restless, almost primitive second-guessing of the enemy, with his ruthless willpower and pride, his blue eyes, his vivid cursing, the kindness of his heroism. *Vanya-Communist* also died. The guns on the destroyers, which had used up their ammunition, had practically none left and the promised back-up supplies never arrived.

Then at dusk a motor boat removed the tarpaulin from four dark oblong objects, set out in rows. The mine layers, the flagship navigator and the commander, deliberated for a long time, leaning over the map, and when they left the office, they were silent and shook hands especially tightly. The fleet commander escorted four sailors and an officer to the deck, and a few minutes later the destroyer, loaded with underwater 'Ribka' mines, disappeared behind the island.

It returned in the morning. The long black mines - which looked like buckets with big moustaches - were no longer visible on the stern. Now there was one thing left: to wait quietly. And, indeed, on the second day, the Whites – who were rejoicing at the destruction of the *Vanya-Communist* with all-round drunkenness - went on the offensive.

They set out in a straight line ahead, solemnly, as if they were on parade. For the first time, the commander of the White Guards flotilla - Admiral Stark himself - personally took part in the campaign. His flag was raised on the *Eagle*. But they'd hardly made it beyond Green Island, when the solemn procession was brought to a halt. The gunboat *Labour*, which led the way, suddenly stopped, and its prow was literally torn off the hull: the mines had done their job.

Now on the icy shores of Kama, lie the destroyed and charred remains of two gunboats: the *Vanya-Communist* and the White Guard *Labour,* almost next to each other. And who knows, it may even be that, beneath the surface, Markin and those despicable adversaries who finished off his drowning team with machine guns, will be intertwined on the dark riverbed.

Leaving Kama, perhaps for the last time, the sailors bid each other long-winded and reluctant farewells. Nothing brings people closer together than jointly experienced dangers, sleepless nights on the bridge, and those extended but excruciating efforts of will and spirit, which prepare and make possible a victory. Most of this goes unnoticed from the outside.

There is no history which reflects upon and appreciates the great and small feats performed daily by the sailors of the Volga Military Flotilla. The names of those who by their voluntary discipline, their intrepidity and modesty helped to create a new fleet are hardly even known.

Of course, individuals do not make history. However, in Russia we had so few people and characters of this calibre, by and large. It was so difficult for them to break through the undergrowth of old and new bureaucracy that they rarely found themselves in the real-life, life-and-death struggle – not the one fought with words on paper. And it's because the Revolution had men like this, men in the highest sense of the word, that Russia is able to rally and recover.

And there's no shortage of these men. Among the milieu I witnessed, there were many of them. At decisive moments they stood out from the general mass, and all of them displayed an authority - a full, genuine authority. They were aware of their heroic task and by their actions were able to rouse the rest of the wavering and pliable masses.

For example, here is the easy-going Yeliseyev, a man of few words and a wonderful gunner. He was the one who hit a boat at a twelve-mile distance from a long-range gun. With his blue eyes, and no eyelashes – singed every time the gun discharges - always fixed upon somewhere far in the distance.

Or there's Babkin. Despite the fact that he's very ill and has not long to live – his eyes glaze over in the heat, like a drunk– he nevertheless dispenses the treasures of his carefree, kind and incomprehensibly steadfast spirit as if he were a Tsar. He's the one who prepared the minefield for the Whites, the one which blew up their most powerful gunboat *Labour*.

Then there's Nikolay Nikolaevich Struisky, the flagship navigator and the person in overall charge of operations in the second half of the campaign on the River Kama. He is one of the very best specialists and most educated of the sailors who served Soviet power flawlessly throughout the Civil War. Even though he, along with several junior officers, was forcibly mobilized and almost had to be brought to the front under escort. They arrived, on *Ebb Tide*, hating the Revolution, sincerely believing that the Bolsheviks were German spies, honestly believing every word they read in *Free Speech* or *The Financial Times*.

On the very next morning after they arrived, they took part in a battle. First, there was the grim distrust, the cold rectitude of people who have been forced to take part in someone else's mistaken, offensive business. But as soon as the first shots had been fired, everything changed. It's impossible to employ half measures when the lives of dozens of people who blindly follow all orders depends on one word from the team, as does the existence of the destroyer, this beautiful fighting machine.

An invisible steel thread connects to each sailor from the captain's bridge. His voice commands the machine, its speed, its firepower and the steering wheel, rotating in the trembling hands of the helmsman. A good sailor can't carry out sabotage during a battle. He clears his mind of all politics, he meets fire with fire, he attacks as resolutely as he defends, brilliantly and unflappably carrying out his professional duty. And then, of course, he's no longer free. He is united with the commander, with the team, with the red flag on the mast. He takes pride in a victory, is proudly aware of the need for it, and also knows about the absolute power he presides over – as an officer and an intellectual – in a moment of danger.

After ten days of combat, which usually takes place at close quarters, after the first victory, and after the first solemn meeting, when the workers of some town have been liberated from the Whites, everyone takes off with music to the wharf-side and shakes hands with the sailors, all equally firmly: the first to jump ashore, the pampered, aristocratic fingers of the unwilling 'Red Officer', not daring yet to believe that he is also a comrade, a member of the 'united army of labour', which is being fan-fared so excitedly, ineptly and joyfully by the provincial brass band playing the Internationale.

All of a sudden, this specialist, this Imperial Service captain of the first rank realises with horror that his eyes are welling up, that all around him is not a 'gang of German spies', but all of Russia, which perpetually calls upon his experience, his academic knowledge, his years of ponderous mental exertions. Someone gives a speech. Oh, it's one of those rude, bullying, illiterate, speeches, which even a week ago would not have aroused anything but a wry smile. Now, the top rank captain listens to it with a beating heart, with trembling hands, afraid to admit to himself that the Russia of these women, deserters and children, of the agitator Comrade Abram,[31] of its men and its Soviets; now it has become his Russia, for which he has fought and would fight for to the end, not being ashamed of her lice, her hunger and mistakes, still not yet knowing, but feeling that only with her will there be justice, a good life and a future.

A week later, wearing a clean collar, with the charcoal and powdery soot washed off his head and face, and all fastened up with the gold buttons, still with the embossed eagles, on his tunic – he hasn't had time yet either to disguise the dark traces and stitching of where his epaulettes had been – he goes to see Comrade Struisky, to explain himself with his Bolshevik superiors. He speaks – tightly gripping the arms of the chair like you do when the ship is rolling.

'First of all, I don't believe that you, and Lenin, and the rest of the sealed wagon took money from the Germans.'

There's a pause, as though a fusillade has just been fired. Somewhere in the distance, the marine corps are at dinner on the *Standard* kitted out in their golden regalia from the Great War – there are explosions, and a wreck. It's late October.

'Second, Russia is with you, and we are also with you. I will say the same to all the younger comrades who wish to know my opinion. And third, yesterday we took Yelabuga.[32] On the shore, as you know, I found up to a hundred peasant hats. Their brains were splattered all over the riverbank. You've seen it yourself – shoes, leggings, blood. We're half an hour late. This must never be allowed to happen again. You can go at night. Of course – it's a dangerous channel, it's possible to be ambushed in full view of an emplacement ...Nevertheless,

He takes a scribbled-on book out of his pocket. It's called *The Actions of the River Flotillas during the War of the Northern and Southern States.*

✪ THE SUMMER OF 1919

One

The offensive began.

After the fighting, the flotilla units came so close together that they were able to communicate non-stop on the radio. Ships live an intense, secret life because they spend so much of their time at sea. Daily campaigns - most of all the siege of Tsaritsyn, which turned out to be especially brutal - are conducted entirely on your own, as if in a dream. The main saving grace is – the marine charts of the Caspian Sea, over which silent hours of introspection flow in the evenings.

This map is not like the usual river charts - the waters are indicated on it by the smooth, wavy lines of currents, stars for lighthouses and innumerable symbols, notifications and forewarnings. The Caspian is very deep, as the simple black and white lines signify. They also follow the meandering features of the shoreline, the treacherous shallows, rapid tides racing from one landmark to another and, finally, the bottomless trenches which sink to an immeasurable depth – while, on the surface, it's as quiet as a lake. How many times have we allowed our imaginations to meander through them, without getting as much as a toe wet?

The dim light from a lamp picks out faces. Flat on the table – the chart's become a chessboard. The players can choose a partner who is hundreds of miles away, on the other side of the meridian: in Baku, Port-Petrovsky or Emba.

Sometimes the eyes of the operators in command fog over at the thought of potential moves. Sometimes, there's a blush on the temples of the schemers: from among thousands of possible moves they sense victory, then gnawing doubts when confronted with two equivalent moves, before settling on an enticing easily accessible entrance to a safe, azure-blue Persian bay.

There are some hypothetically insoluble predicaments...

Then the good ship *Flying Dutchman*[33] appears on the waves, the impossible becomes possible, obstacles disappear, the fog melts, and an audacious move with the rook puts the white king in check.

In anticipation of the impending campaign, the old sailors smoke a lot and don't say much. They smile in the face of the unknown and write long letters home. The young ones experience a particularly special elation, bursting with life.

There will be long days with no shoreline in sight, without a woman, which is why the thought of summer seems especially glorious: walking waist-high through a vineyard, immersed in full-grown rye-corn up to her wavy curls. The night is never fuller than when it is full of stars, the steppe never bloomed whiter and more intoxicating than under a blanket of tiny dry flowers, and the blood never pulsated more thrillingly than it does in time with a galloping horse.

The sea has taken the place of the steppe. The sun bakes, the golden-chestnut stallion breathes easily and runs free, the wind pulls the bronze mane back from its wild eyes and, like the movements of a swan, its great strides rock me to sleep.

Oh, the sea: the deep blue sea!

Two

An infinite number of stories have been written about the sea. It's as all-embracing as poetry, has more resonance than celebrity, and there isn't a single person whose fatigue and sadness would not dissolve in its endless expanses. Everything is left behind as soon as the constant turbulence of the river suddenly merges into the all-conquering swell of the Caspian Sea.

It's night. There's one remarkably bright star in the cold night sky and the moon is surrounded by exceptionally white developing clouds. The Volga flows directly into the Caspian Sea, its entire width opening out, fed by thousands of tributaries whose upper reaches vanish in the mists. Sometimes a snow-white sailboat will pass by on its swallow wings, investigating the shoreline, where no boats of infiltrators should be allowed to slip through.

Sometimes the propeller gets tangled up in the fishing nets and drags them behind like algae - if the bosun is oblivious to this boat, it'll be heading off with his catch.

No one is sleeping. Moonlight illuminates easily recognisable figures. The machine gunner with the black moustache, the back of the crew-cut head of the flag officer, and the usually inert, broad face of the bosun, now gripped by longing for the sea. A handsome young sea-cadet squats down on his haunches and also dreams: likewise, about the sea.

Only a narrow strip of the Caspian belongs to us. But even this strip, where the entire flow of the Volga cannot drown out the salty bitterness of the tide, is enough to intoxicate you forever.

Very slowly, from far in the distance, the day begins.

Ships begin to become visible on the sea for many miles, rising up like phantoms, appearing like motionless far-off islands. Black. Like a rockface, a floating gun-battery; nearby a cluster of schooners, more are dotted about on the horizon in the haze.

Whenever a warship pitches and rolls, the huge iron deck

remains extraordinarily unmoved, the middle of it barely responds.

Tea steams in tin mugs, which the sailors pick up slowly and clasp sheepishly in their hands. Almost two hours of an imperceptible voyage – the night fatigue gradually slips away on a uniform slope. There is apprehension due to being surrounded by water on every side. Drowsiness softens the remaining harshness of its outlines, until it seems that the headboard on the bed is piloting the assault.

The nervous tension affects everybody. It's bound to influence any thinking person aware of why they are making this sea voyage in the early morning and who knows full well that they still have two more hours when they can rest quietly, hang laundry on the stove, smoke a cigarette, and doze off. But their faces are quietly tense, like a smile in the middle of a bad dream.

At the prow of the old ships, when they tack into a turn and rise high above the water, the waves normally break and slam over only in a storm, the spray taking on the shapes of figures who look as though they have been carved from a tree: like water nymphs, or eagles, or Holy Virgins, whose hands and folds of their robes have kept the ship from misfortune. This is what they appear as in the sailor's eyes, which are fixed motionless on the distance. It's an expression of willpower, as though it was frozen like that for all time.

Finally, the alarm sounds, and silhouettes of enemy ships can be seen in the distance, as well as the skeleton of their gunboat which had been hit by a mine.

The atmosphere becomes remarkably relaxed and festive, there are no more tricky meanders in the river, with their potential for an ambush and restricted passage. The Whites are out in the open and we can plainly observe their movements. Three moving shapes turn around – heavy and lumbering, much the same as our own floating fortress, obstinately holding their fire and coaxing an approach.

Further over to the right, the smoke from four more can be seen on the horizon. That makes seven White warships altogether to four Reds. We stop – the artillery duel begins. The Whites are worried; our first volley generates smoke from their stern. What they don't know is that today's gunfire is being directed by a modest, nondescript man, with the blond, single-minded head of a thinker. His entire life is focused on the ship. All the sensitivity and creativity of his youth, consumed by poverty and study, centres on these guns, on their range and their accuracy, on every subtle nuance and idiosyncrasy they have.

The Whites respond well. One of the enemy ships appears to be carrying six-inch guns. Three mighty blasts hit the side of our ship. A large shoal of dead fish sparkle on the water and splinters twinkle. Then we hear the belated howl and whistling noise of bursting air.

A week later, when the aloof Sovolev wasn't on the gun-deck, the commander of the *Hadji-Hadji* brought his ship alongside. He was an old sailor with eleven years of experience called Eliseyev. His ship had been hit thirty-nine times and he'd knocked out one of the Whites' guns. The captain, with shrapnel in his side, never left the bridge. He was carried away, dying.

We set off again in a sea fog. It is next morning before we emerge from it to see warm cheerful land.

Three

Edgar Allan Poe's book *The Raven* was written during the worst period of his life. A black crow flew through a window and then perched on the marble ledge in his Palladian mansion. The raven is a symbol of infinity, a noble witness to grief, a hermit and a judge.

But since then, as a more advanced and better life has

escaped from the gothic cabinet of ideas first to the street and then on to the suburbs - we no longer hear its sublime, piercing cry. The orphaned crow spread out its night wings, edged with touches of grey, flies away between the folds of the constantly flapping curtains and disappears into the morning twilight. On a ploughed field, among the wet clumps of earth, over which the ash-grey filaments of early autumn are already hovering and the mist is lifting - the crow has decided to go for a long walk, alone and silent.

Firmly adjusting his strong legs, tilting his head to the right, then to the left, he walks on the arable field like the 'lord of all he surveys' and has no interest in the lowly, earthly fare.

Sometimes a hoarse screech bursts from its purple throat, making the morning breeze seem colder. The ignorant countryside birds don't dare to answer. 'Nevermore!', the raven exclaims - 'Nevermore!' This is the cry of the monk in a black cassock who does not believe in the great changes and liberation of the prisoner, whose solitary confinement he has gloatingly observed for many a long night. And, waving his forbidding wings he flies south with a croak, like a burst of laughter, and a strange, gurgling, billing and cooing.

The crow has reached a sad city, located where the blue river flows into the dead sea, hopelessly closed in by land on all sides. The heat, and the smell of summer sap his weary body. Black as coal, he approaches the yellow-green water.

Here, in the easy-going realm of incoming and outgoing tides, fishing nets and reeds, seagulls rule the roost. All day long, they cut the milky air with a plaintive cry and with their narrow, curved wings, just like a new-born month. Their eyes glisten like black pearls in white and pink shells. With the tips of their webbed feet, they touch the water, then fly away, dropping a shred of fish or a torn rosary spray.

Now the raven is like the black king in exile, like a piece of coal among flying flakes of snow, or the fragment of a pirate banner carried by the north wind. Wearily and hesitantly flapping it blue-grey wings, the raven mingles with a carefree flock of petrels. Descending to the waterside in a predatory fashion, as he would have done previously landing on the cross of a gravestone or the cross-beam of a scaffold, he stretches his sharp claws, treading as in ancient times in the wise books of magicians. The raven pecks at the mirror of the waters, but seeing beneath him a fluid, transparent, invincible element, hastily recoils with bewilderment and malice.

The seagulls cry and laugh, intoxicated by their non-stop flight, as they sway in mid-air, plunge with insane speed, then rise up again on angels' wings. The raven fights hard among them, and searches the sky with hungry eyes, high up into the distance.

'Nevermore!' the raven shouts. 'Nevermore!' and takes off, goaded – like his conscience.

There, where the sunset glows ominously over the burning sands, where the presence of rare poisonous butterflies are a harbinger of nightfall, where the battle continued all day on the fractured shores in the dust and intense heat and horses without riders bolt, champing at the bit, to swim to the opposite shore – this is the new domain of the raven. Its wings commend the faint-hearts of the fugitives who abandoned their guns. When they light fires on the marshy islands, humiliated and hungry and praying for salvation, he shouts down to them from above: 'Nevermore!'

An expanding flock joins him on the killing fields, sensing death itself in the raven's cry. Hundreds, thousands of birds congregate in an ugly cloud. They fly low, searching for prey, then spread out over their handiwork in the form of a writhing worm, a predatory caterpillar. It spreads out like a black shawl passing through a brooch and, in air which is thick with the smell of decay, follows the invisible path taken by bullets.

From the shoreline where the exodus began, boats full of holes and full of water drift in the current. The heads of the dead bend over the sides. The night engulfs them, the water laps at the flowing blood, and the river, the good boatman of Eternity, transports them through the black Styx and consigns them to distant shallows.

And when they are found in the morning, and their hearts beat again and their eyelids are raised – an angry crow flies away and shouts in the face of the sun: 'Nevermore!'

Four

I am Zhelikovky's wife.

A small piece of ice melts in a flash and finally, light, easing tears come.

The wife. On her face, on her red, inflamed eyelids, on her hair, tousled under a white handkerchief, on her entire being, the still quivering imprint and breath of a great friend, who died, who was killed in action. Her eyes are wide-open and sunken, beneath her broad forehead, on an inexplicably thin lens it is not yet possible to blot out the memory of his appearance as he left early in the morning, before dawn, full of dread forebodings, for some reason leaving his poor sailor's breakfast untouched on the table.

And even her voice, even her voice is like a sharp and direct reprimand, in a high throaty tenor, which her loved one involuntarily learned to mimic.

Now Zhelikovsky's wife is almost as one with him: these are his hands, which stretched out of the water appealing for help. These are his eyes blinded by fire; his head, which he gripped helplessly with his hands; his adorable, fractured head, ready to go to the deep.

Don't talk to her, don't touch her. She is the wife of a hero, one of the best, who died for the RSFSR.[34] Her great grief cannot be helped. She has the courage to live and is not afraid to see his terrible body, slowly floating somewhere adrift in the current, past the wheel of a steamboat.

His wife is calm and knows that, after all, he will be carried out to sea, which he loved. From the confines of a river to this immensity: it's all total nonsense to her.

And I want to suggest an eccentric, unforgiving case: those who have gone, the nearest and dearest, went to their deaths with pride and bravery. It saved them from captivity, from betrayal, from prison. Much better to die in open combat, among comrades, with weapons in their hands. That's how I want to die. That's how Zhelikovsky died, how hundreds and thousands die for this Republic every day.

Five

It's the night before the assault on Tsaritsyn,[35] and now everyone who is still alive is bursting with excitement. What will happen tomorrow is unknown, but today all is well.

Oleanders are blooming in the cramped but clean staff courtyard. This is the old-fashioned, white house where Azin lives and, much against his will, he is buzzing with fierce joy. An irate, rich widow carries tea with a smile in pot-bellied cups. The tall cabinets of gilded glass tremble from the slightest movement; the leaves of houseplants stand out simply and solemnly green against the background of the wide, white-tiled furnaces. It's clean inside too, there's a textured print of the plump couple Adam and Eve in paradise, curtains on the windows, and a chintz coverlet on the bed.

It was essential that, on the eve of the assault, the most decisive brains got together under this roof which was floodlit by a silvery autumn moon in the calm evening sky. Here is the face of Misha Kalinin,[36] shrivelled and crumpled like a used balloon and framed with tufts of hair sticking out like thorns. Then Azin's revitalised head, upon which rests the incredible weight of responsibility, and of the entire Communist Fleet. An hour later, the little house on the moonlit shore, the fast-moving horses of an Asian troika, the road to the river and the last handshakes – it's all taken up time. The sound which stays longest in the memory is the fragile tinkling from the musical box - yes, the musical box belonging to the old codgers in the neighbouring, angrily-locked room. It intruded on the meeting for the entire hour.

And now, when all around is night and the wash behind the stern of the destroyer is boiling over – the box still stands on the table in the empty dining room and, uninterrupted, resounds with its chiming musical refrains. The drum inside is rusty, the key is lost, but it carries on playing happy tunes. And under the crystal lid of the elegant cabinet lurks a whole world of outworn manners and mournful ardour.

All night on the river, there is the insane, menacing music of war. The first ship we encounter is the destroyer *Marx*, which we pass in the fog and darkness. All of the ships pass each other like ghosts. One, two, then another, along the opposite bank, where shells are already falling. The forest ravine is also full of golden flashes. From the depths of the river, thick pillars erupt from the explosions. Sailors anxiously watch the ascent of a major star, flat and white - glowing like a lantern. It is so large and imposing that at first they think it's a signal flare, and send a special lifeboat to put it out.

Ahead of us, the explosions glow red in the mist. It's like watching the door of a red-hot furnace endlessly slamming open and shut. The bombardment turns into that continuous intoxicating rumble which indicates the beginning of the assault. Each ship is shrouded in a powdery veil, and moves towards an enemy which it has hunted down, to challenge it in the dark.

From behind a promontory, a squadron of fighter jets appears, behind them black minesweepers, these knights of the night and the dusk, heading to their posts with visors at half-mast – ominous pursuers of a dead cargo.

By dawn, the gunfire was subsiding. Now, it's time for the army to go on the offensive, and the motor-launch, which has been sent to scout ahead, heading to Tsaritsyn, identifies our first target on a bare-earth summit.

It's hard to write about it. You need to witness these dark figures, who have taken a kicking time and again and who appear so infinitely weak from a distance, heading for the best way out but doomed in advance, regardless of which exit they choose. The sailors can also see them from their ships. Suddenly, someone screams. What? It's okay, he's just short of breath. And the petty officer shouts, not in his usual voice – 'Don't let go, bastard!' The moment it leaves his lips, the anchor chain jumps.

At dawn, the air raids begin. From six in the morning till night-time, there is a continuous hail of bombs, especially on the river. Mainly, these air raids are depressing. But after a sleepless night, after a desperate struggle, when your head reels sweetly and dizzily and everyone calls each other a friendly 'You'. No! It's not terrible.

When the whistle blows twice, it means: 'I see an enemy plane.' One by one, the ships repeat the shrill whistle and lift the anchor. The lottery of failures begins.

There are an average of 4-8 bombs per vessel. You can see them falling, accompanied by a hideous squeal and deafening explosions. One deck or another deck is covered with shrapnel. The *Fearless* was hit on the prow, a commando and three others were wounded, the team rushed to bring the bandages to where the explosion had taken place. Desperately fending off the bombs, she again resumes the attack.

One by one – a light motor-boat, a gun battery, one of the inadequate, wide-bodied first division boats, disappear in a cloud of steam and shrapnel - and miraculously come out of it. The destroyers hotly defend the rest and embroider the sky with white plumes of anti-aircraft fire, with an angry rumbling of their engines, ploughing through a grey moustache of foam, and with their guns slowly and calmly firing, well aware of the impossibility of not being seen.

By the evening, a few solitary figures, clearly blackened, can be seen on the summit. Within an hour, they are already hundreds, and the whole road is covered with fugitives. Our troops take a step back.

Tired horses are led for a reason but they will go well enough, with rifles. The camels, with their habitual obedience and all the grace of mature, elderly women, haul the guns, wagons and people. The assault has not been a success.

The Sisters of Mercy put those who have fallen on the shore onto a sofa in the office. Whenever there are tragedies at sea, strangers like them always arrive unexpectedly and these are just such faces. You will never forget what they look like, no matter how short the meeting. They never disappear, life just moves on.

This girl has a ridiculously squeaky voice. From under the blanket, you can see her tatty boots. One eye, her cheek and her chin are hidden by a bandage. Her round nose is freckled and gashed with scars. What is of most concern and distressing with her is her rasping, unhealthy cough.

She joined her regiment from some remote corner of the Ukraine, barely recovering from her wounds. That's a very long and painful journey. It's an absolute purgatory of long roads, hellish train travel, and a burning fear of forever being separated from all the names and faces which connected her to the Revolution.

Now she's on the banks of the Volga, where the Cuban bonfires now flicker and upon which a wave of humanity involuntarily broke, driven by an unyielding will and an open-hearted, unprocessed purity of the soul. Lying alongside their identity cards are letters from the regiment, which begin with countless greetings, and a stack of letters climbing and teetering up to an enormous height. She looks sideways at these letters, which protrude and tremble like aspen leaves in autumn, with her one blue-grey, darkly speckled eye.

That's how she is: forever disfigured and charming.

The Belarusian doctors, to whom she had at one point crawled after the battle, not knowing who they were, refused to bandage her and - in the name of mercy – dumped her on the street, in the rain, at night. Then she herself, sitting on their porch, without the strength to move, tore something cold away from her face which was blocking her vision - it was her cheek. Fortunately, in the morning, the 'Infirmary' fled, and the poor creature sheltering at the door picked herself up.

The Revolution, whose face no one has ever had the honour to see, should have the same crystal clear blue eye, and maybe a bandage, and on the prominent, rustic lips (lips which kiss simply and coolly) – the pink foam of burst capillaries.

At night, the officer's mess is tidied up with bouquets of red autumn ash, the table is filled with light, and the participants, who have washed the dirt from the trenches or from oily machines off their high boots, quietly confer about the future.

By chance, they are seated like this: on the left, with his sharp eyes, deep bass voice and iron will, sits Shorin. Next to him is his staff officer, a soft-spoken and petite man, who is incapable of ousting anyone, a bit like the survey map which is diligently folded and slung over his shoulder.

Then there is a contorted and pale profile, bent like a sabre, with slightly slanting eyes and an almost smiling mouth. In short, one of those that could pose for an artist as the grand and enduring god of revenge, in a Cossack fur hat. With his silent movements, the faint scent of perfume, which he loved like a woman, this is Khazanov. On his black shirt is the Red Order. He has become almost a legend as the head of the amphibious detachments of the Volga Flotilla.

The Dutch, who achieved perfection in the group portrait, liked to place one determined and slender face in the centre of the picture, among all those gentlemen in black costumes and starched white collars. This would usually be of some glorious young doctor, armed with a scalpel – a sceptic and an atheist – facing the viewer in a half-turn with his high forehead and mocking smile

Here, this figure is now called, 'Mikhailov, Member of the Revolutionary Military Soviet'. He's in a leather jacket and with the tip of *Izvestia*[37] sticking out of his pocket,

Some devil stuck a broken shard of a ragged mirror in Comrade Trifonov. From exile and prison, he carried the intense reserve of a long-term prisoner, a somewhat excruciating fear of voices that are too loud, unrestrained thoughts or characters. As a strong and intelligent man, a magnificent Bolshevik and a soldier of the Revolution, he had no time for those who tried to deceive themselves, or others. The way he saw it, to act the big 'I am' was the most unimpressive, the most vulgar trait a person could have. But cheerful new shoots sprouted through all the holes in logic during the tumultuous year of 1919. The irrepressible winds of time ripped the grey glasses from Trifonov's black face. That doesn't bother him: today he still stubbornly clings to his long-departed mental acuity and cherished underground feeling.

Next - how do you begin to describe Azin? First of all, he's in the wild city of Ogryz, almost cut off from the Kama; he's at a sentry post, lurking along the railway; he's in a stuffy, third-class carriage, filled with the light of ballroom candles from two suspended Gudonov candelabra, appropriated from a ruined manor; he's surrounded by impenetrable cigarette smoke, amid the disturbing restlessness of the HQ, where the commissar of some beleaguered outpost or other - who travelled more than twenty-five miles through enemy defences - has now fallen down on the floor, unconscious, in a deep blissful sleep. His tattered playing cards sticking to tacky tables, drenched in tea and ink. He is on guard holding the black cord of a field phone, dripping wet from the dew of night-time shrubbery, numb from the cold, lack of sleep and the fear of falling asleep while on duty.

Azin uses his spurs to crush the bedbugs in the velvet seats of the carriage. He also used them to personally flog any of the deserters who were caught when they lost the battles at Sarapul

Vladimir Azin, seated, third from the left, hands in his pockets, on the road to Kazan. 7 November 1918.

and dozens of other obstinate cities. He led a crazy, head-on cavalry attack against Tsaritsyn; he made mincemeat of dozens of captive officers and either freed or mobilized thousands of White soldiers. Azin is always full on, does not drink a drop - until it doesn't matter, of course - swears terribly with his own commissars, bypasses the Revolutionary Military Soviet, keeps his own hedgehog and incredibly, was recruited from the river-pirates and Makhno-ites.[38] He fights and never runs. He cries with anger, like a woman, if he even has to take a rest in the midst of the offensive because of a wounded hand.

Nestor Makhno was a Ukrainian anarchist and commander of the Revolutionary Insurrectionary Army of Ukraine between 1917 and 1921. Slogan: 'Death to all those who get in the way of freedom for working people'.

Nestor Makhno

It's Azin himself who arranges a grand get-together. Seeing that on the shore the orchestra is not ready, he warms up in the gunboat behind, so that after another ten minutes, he arrives soaking wet in his magnificent burqa (it's round about July) to accept the honours. The Internationale plays and reports are given by comrades who took part in the victory, buttons are sewn onto everybody's trousers and faces are shaved which haven't been washed for three weeks. This is necessary: without a holiday, without music and a get-together, the army will never get a breather. It has its twenty-four-hour combat birthdays and, without them, it will not move on to the upcoming battles in the morning.

It's Azin who takes his whip to his brazen and much-loved batman for stealing a piglet from the peasants. And it's Azin who walks like a beast, who spends whole nights, nights that are blacker than soot, with music, with vodka and women - but of course, also makes sure that all the barriers are erected and sentries posted, that the intelligence is sent, makes sure that the city is taken, and blocked from all sides. Put simply, almost every day, Azin leads his units into battle, never thinking that he is their leader and has no right to risk his own life.

But Azin pokes about on his map like an unfrozen patch of water probing just beneath the surface of the ice. He listens out in the same way that Vasily Shorin might do, climbing out of the machinery with a long strip of insulating tape, tapping away with a hammer, at the same time as issuing direct and precise orders, with a very distinctive turn of phrase and that calm, superb rudeness with which Old Shorin was able to speak to those whom he loved, whom he was either exhorting forward or insisting on retreat, with an iron operational bridle.

What can you say to someone like Azin? He loved, passionately loved his units. He loved and understood every recruit who had been taken from under their parents' skirts - a young man with protruding ears under an exorbitant forage cap, in a cloak down to the heels, and with only one thought: where to position a heavy-duty gun? With kids like this he was able to fight, to co-ordinate victories. Although they might be starving or laid low by typhoid, they fought from one end of Russian to the other, so that after – after the battles on the River Kama and the Volga, after Tsaritsyn and Saratov – it was absurd that he should perish at Prokop almost on the day after his capture, and die being maligned by the Whites, who spread rumours about his treason towards the Red Army.

This Azin was a hero, a soldier, a weapon. He fought in such a way that he forged an entire Division with his bare hands. So much so that miracles were performed by both soldiers and commissioners. After his death, the 28th Division became the Azinsky Division, and on the dusty squares of Baku, and in Georgia, and on the Persian border, they followed his old marching step in his motley, raggedy breeches with the general's stripes on the sides, simply and resolutely sitting on their diminutive horses, and recruited from Perm to Astrakhan.

On this evening at tea the company begin an argument about heroism. It's an odd theme among people who have long been accustomed to war and most of them having already been decorated with all manner of insignia.

The sceptic in the leather jacket, stirring in his glass with a spoon, calmly dismissed any romantic notions in the cause of the Revolution which had become his craft. The distinctive feature of the intellectual is that, having been cured of phraseology at the front, he gradually recovers and grows up, happy that he can finally submit to the mighty and simple engines of life without looking back or harbouring any doubts. A sense of duty, brotherly solidarity, obedience and sacrifice become a healthy habit. And, afraid to lose this still fragile internal balance, the intellectual, who became a soldier of the Revolution, plants his feet firmly on the ground and endlessly repeats to himself a reassuring 'two times two equals four'.

Listening to the smart commissar, the soldier in the general's epaulettes popped an extra piece of sugar in his glass, with downcast eyes. Lately, in among his well-marked maps and his emphatic orders, the same kind of theoretical discussions have been droning on for half the night, the essence of which he poorly understood, but with the unconscious wisdom of the old military man, flew in the face of all his own experience with each passing hour.

He is wearing the Red Order on his chest. He is proud of it and, reading the reports from the front, senses between the lines the same intense desire for victory as he himself feels. No matter which way you looked at it, it is impossible to apply that ideological middle-of-the-road, dreary equivocation and admiration for everyday life, which now, sitting before Shorin, in a smooth voice shattered some pure, exalted, celebratory aspect of his thought.

Azin has not yet lost the proud blush of shame from his face, for some minor defeat at the front, something he has often repeated in front of so many strangers. Likewise, Kalinin, is tired hearing about his own truly fearless bravery, which he considers the duty of a Communist and a commissar. They both hesitated to speak, enjoying a cigarette and the case someone is arguing, but saying nothing.

But the grating speech more and more fractures the atmosphere of lightness and peace in the room, generally rare in these places. It may seem strange that a normal existence, which after each and every danger should appear more attractive and appealing, seems so dull and dreary to the likes of Shorin, who is prepared to sacrifice his own brains and treat that with contempt in a fit of cold curiosity.

Especially for Azin, his legs still hurt from the saddle, all over his body spilled sweet fatigue from autumn, from red and gold trees, from the green meadows, blooming with the last brightness, from the kind eyes and smooth gait of camels, enticing wagons piled high with reeds through the steppe. In the morning he had almost been killed during the reconnaissance, but by the evening so much serene earth, fresh air and the bitter, exciting smells of autumn.

And such tenderness - he could not remember who it had to do with: was it the sailors he had met on the shore, who had come from the Tsarist prison with scars on their bodies, or to the letters which had arrived so late and from so far away? Then, suddenly, someone is sitting here, denying the essence of life, its miracles and marvellous arbitrariness. Someone who denies heroism.

'So, you…', Azin glimpses a warning in someone's eyes and because of that does not swear.

I wanted to take the map, find on it the red wreath of the Republic, which for two years bloomed alone in the world and which was heroically defended by an exhausted and backward population. When was life more wonderful than during these great years? If you don't see anything now, don't feel relief. Rather the wrath and the glory which imbue even the most miserable, the most desperate day of this unique struggle in history, than to live and die in the name of what exactly?

Notes

1   Larissa Reisner began her studies in the Faculty of Law and Philology at St Petersburg University in 1912 and also trained in Psychoneurology at the Bekhterev Research Institute.

2   Poem by Vladimir Mayakovsky from the collection Для Голоса (*For the Voice*). 1923

3   Russian abbreviation of the name for the higher education preparatory schools known as the Рабочий Факултет, or Workers' Faculty.

4   Class of destroyers which formed part of the Russian navy's Baltic Fleet but were transferred to operations on the River Volga during the Civil War. Larissa Reisner's husband, Feodor Raskolnikov, was Admiral-of-the-Fleet.

5   Following the October Revolution in Russia and the agreement drawn up at the Treaty of Brest-Litovsk to end Russian participation in the First World War, a split developed in the Czech army. Till then, the Czechs had enthusiastically participated in the war against Germany and the Austro-Hungarian Empire. Subsequently, some joined forces with the Red Army, others – many of them based in the Ukraine – continued to support the Allied forces and became the vanguard of the anti-Bolshevik forces for many months.

6   Sviyazhsk, in present-day Tatarstan, is an outpost located on the western banks of the River Volga, a few miles from the naval base at Kazan but on the opposite shore. It is often referred to as an island but is connected to the mainland by a causeway and a bridge. Sviyazhsk railway station is located 6 kilometres west of the island and is linked to the settlement at Sviyazhsk with a highway which runs along the causeway. Population: 238

7   The Old Believers are members of a branch of the Eastern Orthodox Christian faith who broke away from the established orthodoxy in 1652, following the introduction of reforms to religious rites and practices instituted by the Patriarch Nikon. The Old Believers maintained that the official church had fallen into the hands of the Antichrist. They were subsequently anathemised and suppressed both by by the church and by the state. By the time of the Russian Revolution, communities established by the Old Believers were most prevalent in Lithuania, Ukraine and Romania. Russians often refer to the 17th century split as the раскол (raskol - or split) and describe to the adherents of the old orthodoxy, in a derogatory fashion, as the раскольники (raskolniks - splitters, or schismatics). This is the same name used by Dostoevsky to describe his fictional protagonist, Rodion Raskolnikov, in *Crime & Punishment* – and is also the pseudonym chosen by Larissa Reisner's husband, Fyodor Raskolnikov. His real name was Fyodor Ilyin.

8   Kronstadt is a man-made fortification and naval base which guards the entrance to St Petersburg. It is also the headquarters of the Baltic Fleet.

9   Fyodor Fyodorovich Raskolnikov married Larissa Reisner in the summer of 1918. He was born, Fyodor Ilyin, in St Petersburg in 1892, the son of a general's daughter and an orthodox priest. He joined the Bolsheviks in 1910 and worked on the Bolshevik newspaper, *Pravda*. Arrested and then exiled, first to Germany, then to Arkhangel, he enlisted in the navy in 1917 and was sent as a midshipman to the sea fortress at Kronstadt, where he continued his revolutionary activities. He was one of

the organisers of the Kronstadt Mutiny in July 1917. In November of the same year, he was sent to fight anti-Bolshevik insurgents in Moscow and soon after was elected to the Russian Constituent Assembly. In July 1918, he was sent to Kazan as Commissar of the Revolutionary Military Soviet on the Eastern Front and commanded the Red Volga Flotilla, which participated in the Kazan operation. Raskolnikov became a prisoner of war when his destroyer, *Spartak,* was captured by the Royal Navy off the coast of Estonia. He was held in Brixton prison until May 1919, when he was exchanged for 17 British prisoners of war. Appointed commander of the Caspian Flotilla, he led the assault on the British base at Enzeli (in present-day Iran). The attack destroyed what remained of the White Russian navy.

10   In the original text, Larissa Reisner, refers to this woman as the 'wife of Comrade Sheiman' but she is evidently referring to herself.

11   See previous note. In the original, this sentence reads: 'The realisation dawns on her ashen, stony face: Sheiman has been killed, without a doubt.'

12   Also known as the Khan's Mosque, a multi-tiered leaning tower which was once the highest structure in the Kazan Kremlin. According to legend, the Kazan tatar queen Söyembikä threw herself from the tower when she was detained by Muscovite forces, led by Ivan the Terrible.

13   Novel written by Maxim Gorky in 1909, exposing the autocratic police system and the decay of the bourgeoisie in Russia, combined with an affirmation of revolutionary ideas.

14   Boris Kustodiev was a leading figure in the art movement known as Мир Искусства (Mir Iskusstva – World of Art). He illustrated many works of Russian literature, including those by Gogol, Lermontov and Tolstoy.

15   In the election to the Russian Constituent Assembly held two weeks after the October Revolution in 1917, the party with the largest number of votes was the Socialist Revolutionaries (SRs) whose base was among the peasantry. However, the SRs were divided between those who supported the Bolsheviks (the Left SRs) and those who opposed them (the Right SRs). The combined votes of the Bolsheviks and the Left SRs gave them a majority. After the Bolsheviks disbanded the Constituent Assembly in January 1918, since it had been superseded in reality by Soviet democracy among the workers and the peasantry, the SRs lost their political significance. For a short period, in some parts of the country - including Kazan - some SRs sided with the counter-revolutionary forces led by Admiral Kolchak of the Whites and the Czech Legions. In Kazan and the surrounding area, they threatened to form an alternative government to the Bolsheviks – which declared 'All Power to the Constituent Assembly' - and to declare Kolchak as the 'Supreme Leader and Commander-in-Chief of All Russian Land and Sea Forces'. In August 1918, the Whites occupied Kazan and shot every Bolshevik they found who had remained in the city.

16   Count Alexey Arakcheev was a Russian general during the reign of Alexander I, notorious for the brutal regime he introduced in the army and for the establishment of military-agricultural colonies. His methods became a byword for extreme repression known as the 'Arakcheevshchina'.

17   The Order of the Red Banner was established on 28 December 1920 to reward distinguished exploits.

18   Ivan Nikitich Smirnov joined the RSDLP in 1899, at the age of 18. In

August 1917, he was organiser of the Bolshevik publishing house Вольна (Volna – Wave) in Moscow and a deputy on the Constituent Assembly. During the Civil War he was a member of the Revolutionary Military Council on the Eastern Front. He played a pivotal role in the defeat of Admiral Kolchak during the Civil War. He was a close associate of Grigory Zinoviev and, from 1923, a member of Trotsky's Left Opposition to Stalin. He was expelled from the Communist Party in 1927 and sentenced to three years in exile. In 1933 he was sentenced to 5 years in the labour camps, then brought to trial as a defendant in the 'United Anti-Soviet Trotskyite-Zinovievite Centre' and sentenced to death in August 1936 (rehabilitated in 1988).

19   Mikhailov was one of the pseudonyms used by Mikhail Vasilyevich Frunze, a leading Bolshevik during the Russian Revolutions of 1905 and 1917. He became a Red Army commander during the Civil War and is best known for defeating the White Army led by Alexander Kolchak in Omsk and then in the Crimea, led by Baron von Wrangel. Frunze's support for Zinoviev brought him into conflict with Stalin. Frunze died during surgery in 1927. There were rumours that Stalin had ordered his death. A report published in *Izvestia* in 2010 claimed that Frunze had died as the result of a massive overdose of chloroform.

20   Joachim Vicietis was a Latvian military commander. During World War I, he was colonel of the 5th Latvian Zemgale Rifle Regiment which supported Lenin's Bolsheviks after the October Revolution and then during the Civil War. Though he never joined the Communist Party, he worked closely with Trotsky and from April 1918 he was commander of the Red Latvian rifle division, then commander of the Eastern Front. In November 1937, at the height of Stalin's Great Purge, Vicietis was arrested and accused of being a member of a Latvian Fascist Organisation. He was executed in July 1938 (and rehabilitated in 1957).

21   Boris Savinkov was a Left SR and the son of a Tsarist prosecutor. In 1904, he took part in the assassination of the Minister of Internal Affairs, Viacheslav Plehve, and the Grand Duke, Sergey Alexandrovich. Following a period in exile, he returned to Russia and became deputy war minister in Kerensky's government. After the October Revolution, he pledged to overthrow the Bolsheviks with the support of former Tsarist officers and the French. He organised a series of armed uprisings against, all of which were defeated. He then joined the Russian émigré community in Paris and eventually became Admiral Kolchak's main representative. He was an acquaintance of the British secret agent, Sidney Reilly, and was involved in a number of counter-revolutionary plots against the Bolsheviks. He was later lured back to Moscow where – according to the NKVD – he committed suicide by jumping from a window of the Lubyanka, HQ of the secret police since the times of Catherine the Great.

22   During the summer of 1918, Colonel V O Kappel launched a series of successful raids against the Reds, combining small detachments of land forces with a fleet of river boats. He took part in the seizure of the key cities of Ufa and Simbirsk, the birthplace of Lenin, before the end of July and then drove the Bolsheviks from Kazan – ancient capital of the Tatars until Ivan the Terrible's historic victory over them in 1552.

23   Named after Vladimir Martinovich Azin, commander of the 28th Infantry Division during the capture of Sarapul.

24   In Slavic mythology, the Leshy is a forest demon which can play tricks on people and can be heard in the forest laughing, whistling or singing. It has a human

body from the waist up and the horns, ears and beard of a she-goat.

25   The White River, in present-day Bashkortostan, is a tributary of the River Kama.

26   The *Vanya-Communist* (Ваня-Коммунист) was a paddle-steamer and tugboat converted to a gunboat with the addition of front and rear cannons on the deck

27   Legendary Russian rebel and popular 17th century outlaw, famed for robbing barges loaded with valuables for the rich.

28   Named after the Bolshevik, Semyon Roshal, in 1917.

29   Named after V. Volodarsky (born Moisei Goldstein) a member of the Jewish Bund and editor of the *Red Gazette* in Petrograd.

30   Named after Nikolai Markin, Bolshevik sailor

31   *Comrade Abram* was a pro-Bolshevik TV film produced by E. Ermolev in 1919.

32   Yelabuga: Town on the right bank of the Kama River, 200 kilometres east of Kazan, in present-day Tatarstan.

33   Legendary ghost ship which can never make port and is doomed to sail the oceans forever.

34   RSFSR: Russian Soviet Federation of Socialist Republics.

35   City on the west bank of the River Volga named Tsaritsyn during the Imperial era, between 1589 and 1925. Name changed to Stalingrad between 1925 and 1961, then renamed as Volgograd to the present day.

36   Mikhail Ivanovich Kalinin was a peasant-turned-metal-worker who replaced Sverdlov as Chairman of the All-Russian Central Committee of the Soviets in 1919. Known for his gift for speaking to the Russian peasantry, he spent nine months in the countryside around Kazan in 1919.

37   Meaning *The News,* began its life as the news bulletin of the Petrograd Soviet on 13 March 1917.

38   Nestor Makhno was a Ukrainian anarchist and commander of the Revolutionary Insurrectionary Army of Ukraine between 1917 and 1921. Slogan: 'Death to all those who get in the way of freedom for working people'.

Portrait of Trotsky in his Red Army uniform

✪ TWO EXTRACTS FROM *MY LIFE*: LEON TROTSKY

A Month at Sviyazhsk

The spring and summer of 1918 were unusually hard. All the aftermath of the war was then just beginning to make itself felt. At times it seemed as if everything were slipping and crumbling, as if there were nothing to hold to, nothing to lean upon. One wondered if a country so despairing, so economically exhausted, so devastated, had enough sap left in it to support a new régime and preserve its independence. There was no food. There was no army. The railways were completely disorganized. The machinery of state was just beginning to take shape. Conspiracies were being hatched everywhere.

In the west the Germans occupied Poland, Lithuania, Latvia, White Russia and a large section of Great Russia. Pskov was in their hands. The Ukraine became an Austro-German colony. On the Volga in the summer of 1918 agents of France and England engineered a rebellion of Czecho-Slovak regiments, made up of former war prisoners. The German high command let me know, through their military representatives, that if the Whites approached Moscow from the east, the Germans would come from the west, from the direction of Orsha and Pskov, to prevent the forming of a new eastern front. We were between hammer and anvil.

In the north the French and English occupied Murmansk and Archangel, and threatened an advance on Vologda. In Yaroslavl there broke out an insurrection of the White Guards, organized by Savinkov at the instigation of the French ambassador Noulens and the English representative Lockhart, with the object of connecting the northern troops with the Czecho-Slovaks and White Guards on the Volga, by way of Vologda and Yaroslavl. In the Urals Dutov's bands were at large. In the South on the Don an uprising was spreading under the leadership of General Krasnov, then in actual alliance with the Germans. The left Socialist-Revolutionists organized a conspiracy in July and murdered Count Mirbach; they tried at the same time to start an uprising on the eastern front. They wanted to force us into war with Germany. The civil-war front was taking more and more the shape of a noose closing ever tighter about Moscow.

After the fall of Simbirsk, it was decided that I should go to the Volga, where we were facing the greatest danger. I began to get a special train ready – in those days not so simple a matter. Everything was missing, or, to be more exact, no one knew where to find anything. The simplest task became a complicated improvisation. I never imagined then that I would have to live in that train for two years and a half. I left Moscow on 7 August still ignorant of the fall of Kazan the day before; only en route did I hear that very disturbing news, Red units hastily drawn up for service had left their posts without a struggle and had exposed the defences of Kazan. Part of the staff proved to be traitors; the others had been caught off guard and had to run for safety as best they could, under a rain of bullets. No one knew where the commander-in-chief or the other commanding officers were. My train stopped at Sviyazhsk, the nearest sizable station to Kazan. There for a whole month the fate of the Revolution hung again in the balance. That month was a great training school for me.

The army at Sviyazhsk was made up of detachments which had retreated from Simbirsk and Kazan, and of assisting units rushed in from all directions. Each unit lived its own distinct life, sharing in common only a readiness to retreat – so superior were the enemy in both organization and experience. Some White companies made up exclusively of officers performed miracles. The soil itself seemed to be infected with panic. The fresh Red detachments, arriving in vigorous mood, were immediately engulfed by the inertia of retreat. A rumour began to spread among the local peasantry that the Soviets were doomed. Priests and tradesmen lifted their heads. The revolutionary elements in the villages went into hiding. Everything was crumbling; there was nothing to hold to. The situation seemed hopeless.

Here, before Kazan, one could see on a small stretch of land the multiple diversity of the factors in human history, and could draw up arguments against that cowardly historical fatalism which, on all concrete questions, hides behind the passive working of the law of cause and effect, ignoring the while that most important factor – the living and active man. Could much more be needed to overthrow the Revolution?

Its territory was now reduced to the size of the ancient Moscow principality. It had hardly any army; it was surrounded by enemies on all sides. After Kazan would have come the turn of Nizhni-Novgorod from which a practically unobstructed road lay open to Moscow. The fate of the Revolution was being decided here at Sviyazhsk. And here, at the most critical moment, it rested on a single battalion, on one company, on the courage of one commissary. In short, it really was hanging by a thread. And thus, it went, day in and day out.

Despite all this the Revolution was saved. What was needed for that? Very little. The front ranks of the masses had to realize the mortal danger in the situation. The first requisite for success was to hide nothing, our weakness least of all; not to trifle with the masses but to call everything by its right name. The Revolution was still very irresponsible; the October victory had been won very easily. At the same time the Revolution had not removed, by a single stroke, all the hardships that had fostered it. The spontaneous pressure had relaxed. The enemy was gaining its successes through military organization, the very thing we did not have. But the Revolution was achieving it, before Kazan.

The propaganda throughout the country was being fed by telegrams from Sviyazhsk. The Soviets, the party, the trades unions, all devoted themselves to raising new detachments, and sent thousands of communists to the Kazan front. Most of the youth of the party did not know how to handle arms, but they had the will to win, and that was the most important thing. They put backbone into the soft body of the army.

The commander-in-chief on the eastern front was Colonel Vatzetis, who had been in command of a division of Latvian Rifles. This was the only unit left over from the old army. The Latvian farm-hands, labourers, and poor peasants hated the Baltic barons. Tsarism had capitalized this antagonism in the war with the Germans, and the Latvian regiments had been the best troops in the Tsar's army. After the February Revolution they came almost to a man under the Bolshevik influence and played an important role in the October Revolution.

Vatzetis was enterprising, energetic and resourceful. He had distinguished himself during the insurrection of the left

Socialist-Revolutionists. Under his direction light guns were placed in front of the conspirators' headquarters, and two or three volleys, merely to frighten them without casualties, were enough to make them take to their heels. Vatzetis replaced Muravyov after the treason of the adventurer in the east. Unlike the other officers trained at the military academy, he never lost himself in the chaos of the Revolution, but plunged cheerfully in, blowing bubbles, appealing, exhorting, giving orders even when there was little hope of their being carried out.

While other 'specialists' in government service were more fearful of overstepping their authority than of anything else, Vatzetis in his moments of inspiration would issue orders as if the Soviet of Commissaries and the Central Executive Committee did not exist.

About a year later he was accused of dubious schemes and connections and had to be dismissed, but there was really nothing serious about the accusations. Perhaps before going to sleep the chap had been reading Napoleon's biography, and confided his ambitious dreams to two or three young officers. Today, Vatzetis is a professor in the military academy.

In the retreat from Kazan on 6 August he was one of the last to leave the staff headquarters when the Whites were already entering the building. He managed to make his escape and arrived at Sviyazhsk by way of a circuitous route, having lost Kazan but not his optimism. We considered the more important questions together, appointed the Latvian officer Slavin commander of the Fifth army and said good-bye to each other. Vatzetis left for his staff headquarters and I remained at Sviyazhsk.

Among the party workers who arrived on the same train with me was a man named Gusev. He was called an 'old Bolshevik' because of his share in the Revolution of 1905. He had retired to bourgeois life for the next ten years, but, like many others, returned to Revolution in 1917. Later Lenin and I removed him from military work because of some petty intrigues, and he was immediately picked up by Stalin.

His special vocation today chiefly that of falsifying the history of the civil war, for which his main qualification is his apathetic cynicism. Like the rest of the Stalin school he never looks back over what he has done or said before. At the beginning of 1924, when the campaign against me was already quite overt, Gusev played his role of phlegmatic slanderer. But the memory of those days at Sviyazhsk, despite the six intervening years, was still too fresh, and acted as a check on even him. This is what he said then of the events before Kazan:

The arrival of Comrade Trotsky worked a decisive change in the situation. In Comrade Trotsky's train to the obscure station of Sviyazhsk there came a firm will to victory, a sense of initiative, and resolute pressure in all phases of the army work. From the very first days everyone began to feel that some abrupt change had taken place, not only at the station – the active campaign headquarters of the political section and the army supply staff, crammed with the supply trains of countless regiments – but even in army units stationed about fifteen versts away. It was first apparent in the matter of discipline. Comrade Trotsky's harsh methods were most expedient and necessary for that period of undisciplined and irregular warfare. Persuasion counted for nothing, and there was no time for it. And so, during the twenty-five days that Comrade Trotsky spent at Sviyazhsk, a tremendous amount of work was done, with the result that the disorganized and demoralized units of the Fifth army were changed into the fighting units that later recaptured Kazan.

Treason had nests among the staff and the commanding officers; in fact, everywhere. The enemy knew where to strike and almost always did so with certainty. It was discouraging. Soon after my arrival I visited the front-line batteries. The disposition of the artillery was being explained to me by an experienced officer, a man with a face roughened by wind and with impenetrable eyes. He asked for permission to leave me for a moment, to give some orders over the field-telephone. A few minutes later two shells dropped, fork-wise, fifty steps away from where we were standing; a third dropped quite close to us. I had barely time to lie down, and was covered with earth. The officer stood motionless some distance away, his face showing pale through his tan. Strangely enough I suspected nothing at the moment; I thought it was simply an accident.

Two years later I suddenly remembered the whole affair, and, as I recalled it in its smallest detail, it dawned on me that the officer was an enemy, and that through some intermediate point he had communicated with the enemy battery by telephone, and had told them where to fire. He ran a double risk – of getting killed along with me by a White shell, or being shot by the Reds. I have no idea what happened to him later.

I had no sooner returned to my carriage than I heard rifle-shots all about me. I rushed to the door. A White aeroplane was circling above us, obviously trying to hit the train. Three bombs dropped on a wide curve, one after another, but did no damage. From the roofs of our train rifles and machine-guns were shooting at the enemy. The aeroplane rose out of reach, but the fusillade went on – it seemed as if everyone were drunk. With considerable difficulty I managed to stop the shooting. Possibly the same artillery officer had sent word as to the time of my return to the train. But there may have been other sources as well.

The more hopeless the military situation of the Revolution, the more active the treason. It was necessary, no matter what the cost, to overcome as quickly as possible the automatic inertia of retreat, in which men no longer believe that they can stop, face about, and strike the enemy in the chest. I brought about fifty young party men from Moscow with me on the train. They simply outdid themselves, stepping into the breach and fairly melting away before my very eyes through the recklessness of their heroism and sheer inexperience. The posts next to theirs were held by the Fourth Latvian regiment. Of all the regiments of the Latvian division that had been so badly pulled to pieces, this was the worst. The men lay in the mud under the rain and demanded relief, but there was no relief available. The commander of the regiment and the regimental committee sent me a statement to the effect that unless the regiment was relieved at once 'consequences dangerous for the Revolution' would follow.

It was a threat. I summoned the commander of the regiment and the chairman of the committee to my car. They sullenly held to their statement. I declared them under arrest. The communications officer of the train, who is now the commander of the Kremlin, disarmed them in my compartment. There were only two of us on the train staff; the rest were fighting at the front. If the men arrested had showed any resistance, or if their regiment had decided to defend them and had left the front line, the situation might have been desperate. We should have had to surrender Sviyazhsk and the bridge across the Volga. The capture of my train by the enemy would undoubtedly have had its effect on the army. The road to Moscow would have been left open. But the arrest came off safely. In an order to the army I announced the commitment of the commander of the regiment to trial before the revolutionary tribunal. The regiment remained at its post. The commander was merely sentenced to prison.

The communists were explaining, exhorting, and offering example, but agitation alone could not radically change the attitude of the troops, and the situation did not allow sufficient time for that. We had to decide on sterner measures. I issued an

order which was printed on the press in my train and distributed throughout the army:

I give warning that if any unit retreats without orders, the
first to be shot down will be the commissary of the unit,
and next the commander. Brave and gallant soldiers will
be appointed in their places. Cowards, weasels and traitors
will not escape the bullet. This I solemnly promise in the
presence of the entire Red Army.

Of course, the change did not come all at once. Individual
detachments continued to retreat without cause, or else would
break under the first strong onset. Sviyazhsk was open to attack.

On the Volga a steamboat was held ready for the staff. Ten
men of my train crew, mounted on bicycles, were on guard over
the pathway between the staff headquarters and the steamship
landing. The military Soviet of the Fifth army proposed that
I move to the river. It was a wise suggestion, but I was afraid
of the bad effect on an army already nervous and lacking in
assurance. Just at that time the situation at the front suddenly
grew worse. The fresh regiment on which we had been banking
left its post, with its commissary and commander at its head,
and seized the steamer by threat of arms, intending to steam to
Nizhni-Novgorod.

A wave of alarm swept over the front. Everyone began to
look towards the river. The situation seemed almost hopeless.
The staff remained at its post, though the enemy was only a
kilometre or two away and shells were bursting close at hand.
I had a talk with the indispensable Markin. Boarding an improvised gunboat with a score of tested men, he sailed up to
the steamboat held by the deserters, and at the point of a gun
demanded their surrender. Everything depended on that one
moment; a single rifle-shot would have been enough to bring
on a catastrophe. But the deserters surrendered without re-
sisting. The steamboat docked alongside the pier; the desert-

ers disembarked. I appointed a field-tribunal which passed death-sentences on the commander, the commissary, and several privates – to a gangrenous wound a red-hot iron was applied. I explained the situation to the regiment without hiding or softening anything. A number of communists were injected into the regiment, which returned to the battle front with new commanding officers and a new spirit. Everything happened so quickly that the enemy did not have time to take advantage of the disturbance in our ranks.

It was necessary to organize an aviation service. I called up an engineer-pilot. Akashev, who, though an anarchist by conviction, was working with us. Akashev showed his initiative and quickly rounded up an air squadron. At last we got with its help a full picture of the enemy front; the command of the Fifth army had come out of the dark. The fliers made daily air raids on Kazan and a frenzy of alarm took hold of the city. Sometime later after Kazan had been taken, I received some documents that included the diary of a bourgeois girl who went through the siege of Kazan. Pages were given over to descriptions of the panic that our airmen caused, and alternated with pages describing the girl's affairs of the heart. Life went on. Czech officers vied with Russian. Affairs begun in the drawing-rooms of Kazan ran their course and reached their finale in the cellars that served as shelters from the bombs.

On 28 August the Whites launched an outflanking movement. Colonel Kappel, later a celebrated White general, penetrated to our rear under cover of darkness, with a strong detachment behind him, and seized a small railway station, destroyed the tracks, and cut down the telegraph-poles. When he had cut off our retreat in this way, he advanced to attack Sviyazhsk. If I am not mistaken, Kappel's staff included Savinkov.

This move caught us quite off our guard. We were afraid to disrupt the already shaky front, and so we withdrew only two or three companies. The commander of my train again mobilized everyone he could lay his hands on, both in the train and at the station, including even the cook. We had a good stock of rifles, machine-guns and hand-grenades. The train crew was made up of good fighters. The men took their posts about a verst from the train. The battle went on for about eight hours, and both sides had losses. Finally, after they had spent themselves, the enemy withdrew. Meanwhile the break in the connection with Sviyazhsk had stirred up Moscow and the whole line. Small units were rushed to our relief. The line was quickly repaired; fresh detachments poured into the army.

At that time the Kazan papers were reporting that I had been cut off, taken prisoner, killed, had flown away in an aeroplane – but that my dog was captured as a trophy. This faithful animal later was captured on all the civil-war fronts. In most cases it was a chocolate-coloured dog, but sometimes a Saint Bernard. I got off all the cheaper because I never had any dog.

While I was making the rounds of the staff quarters at three o'clock in the morning, on the most critical night at Sviyazhsk, I heard a familiar voice from the staff-room saying: 'He will play this game until he is taken prisoner, and will ruin himself and all of us. You mark my words.' I stopped at the threshold. There, facing me, were two young officers of the general staff, sitting at a table and poring over a map. The man who was speaking stood with his back to me, bent over the table. He must have read something like alarm on his companions' faces, for he turned sharply around towards the door. It was Blagonravov, former lieutenant in the Tsar's army, a young Bolshevik. An expression of mingled terror and shame seemed to freeze on his face.

As a commissary it was his duty to keep up the morale of the specialists attached to the army. Instead of that, here he was, at this critical moment, stirring them against me and actually suggesting that they desert! I had caught him red-handed, and I could scarcely believe my eyes or ears. During 1917 Blagonravov had proved himself a fighting revolutionary. He was the commissary of the Peter-Paul fortress during the Revolution, and later on he took part in the suppression of the military students' uprising. I entrusted him with important commissions during the Smolny period, and he carried them out well. 'Out of such a lieutenant,' I had once said jokingly to Lenin, 'even a Napoleon may come some day. He even has the right name for it: Blago-nravov,* almost like Bona-parte.' Lenin laughed at this unexpected comparison, then he grew thoughtful, and, with his cheek-bones bulging even more, said very seriously, almost threateningly, 'Well, I think we'll manage the Bonapartes, don't you?'

'Everything is in the hands of God,' I answered him in jest. It was this same Blagonravov whom I had sent to the East when the people there had been asleep to the treachery of Muravyov. When, in Lenin's reception-room in the Kremlin, I explained his task to Blagonravov, he answered as if he were depressed: 'The whole point of the thing is that the Revolution has entered upon a decline.' That was in the middle of 1918. 'Is it possible that you are spent so quickly?' I asked him, indignantly. Blagonravov pulled himself up, changed his tone, and promised to do everything that needed to be done. I was reassured. And now I had caught him on the verge of downright treason at our most critical time!

We walked into the corridor so that we need not discuss it in front of the officers. Blagonravov was pale and trembling, with his hand raised to his cap. 'Please don't commit me to the tribunal,' he kept repeating despairingly, I will earn my reprieve if you send me into the lines as a private.' My prophecy had

---

*In Russian this means 'good-natured' or ' good-mannered.'

not come true; here was my candidate for a Napoleon standing before me like a wet hen. He was dismissed from his post and sent to do less responsible work.

Revolution is a great devourer of men and character. It leads the brave to their destruction and destroys the souls of those who are less hardy. Today Blagonravov is a member of the ruling staff of the State Political Board GPU* and one of the pillars of the present régime. He must have learned to hate the 'permanent Revolution' when he was still at Sviyazhsk.

The fate of the Revolution was trembling in the balance between Sviyazhsk and Kazan. No retreat was open, except into the Volga. The revolutionary Soviet of the army informed me that the problem of my safety at Sviyazhsk restricted the freedom of their action and demanded that I move at once aboard a ship on the river. They were entitled to make this demand – from the outset I had made it a rule that my presence at Sviyazhsk should in no way embarrass or restrict the high command of the army. I stuck to this rule all through my stops at various fronts. So, I complied with the demand and moved over to the river, not, however, to the passenger-steamer that had been made ready for me, but to a torpedo-boat.

Four small torpedo-boats had been brought up to the Volga, with great difficulty, by way of the Marinsky canal system. By that time a few of the river steamers also had been armed with guns and machine-guns. The flotilla under the command of Raskolnikov was planning a raid on Kazan that night. It had to pass two high headlands on which the Whites had mounted their batteries. Beyond the headlands the river curved and broadened out, and there the enemy's flotilla was stationed. On the opposite bank Kazan lay open. The plan was to pass the headlands under cover of darkness, destroy the enemy's flotilla

*The GPU, is the abbreviation of 'Gosudarstvennoye Politicheskoye Upravleniye', or 'State Political Directorate', the Soviet secret police.

and shore batteries, and shell the city.

The flotilla set out in battle formation with lights out, like a thief in the night. Two old Volga pilots, both with thin little beards, stood next to the captain. Having been forced to come aboard, they were in mortal fear every minute, and were hating us and cursing their fate, trembling the while like aspens. Now everything depended on them. The captain reminded them from time to time that he would shoot both of them on the spot if they drove the ship aground.

We had just come abreast of the headland, rising dimly out of the dark, when a shot from a machine-gun lashed across the river like a whip. A gunshot followed it from the hill. We went on silently. Behind us, from below, answering shots followed. Several bullets drummed on the iron sheet that protected us to the waist on the captain's bridge. We crouched, and the boat-swains shrank down, searching the darkness with piercing eyes and exchanging words in tense whispers with the captain. Once past the headland we entered the reach. Beyond us on the opposite shore the lights of Kazan were visible. Heavy firing was going on behind us from above and below.

Not more than two hundred yards away at the right, under cover of the hilly banks, the enemy flotilla was lying, the boats looming up as a vague mass; Raskolnikov ordered the guns to open fire on the boats. The metal body of our torpedo-boat groaned and shrieked with the first shot from its own gun. We were moving in jerks, as if that iron womb were giving birth to shells in grinding pain. Suddenly the darkness of the night was stripped naked by a flare – one of our shells had set fire to an oil-barge. An unexpected, unwelcome, but resplendent torch rose above the Volga.

Now we began to fire at the pier. We could see the guns on it clearly, but they did not answer. The gunners apparently had simply fled. The whole expanse of river was lit up. There was no one behind us. We were alone; the enemy's artillery obviously had cut off the passage of the rest of our boats. Our torpedo-boat stood out on that bright river like a fly on a white plate. In another moment we would find ourselves under the crossfire from the headlands and the pier. It gave one the creeps. And on top of this we lost control of our boat. The steering-gear had been broken, probably by a shot. We tried to turn the rudder by hand, but the broken chain got tangled around it and the rudder became useless. We had to stop the engines. The boat was slowly drifting towards the Kazan bank when it ran into an old, half-submerged barge. The firing ceased altogether. It was as light as day and as silent as night. We were in a trap. The only thing that seemed incomprehensible was the fact that we were not being pounded by shells.

We had not realized the destruction and panic caused by our raid. Finally, the young commanders decided to push away from the barge and regulate the movement of the boat by running the right and left engines alternately. It proved successful. With the oil torch still blazing we went on to the headland. There were no shots. Around the headland we sank into darkness again. A sailor who had fainted was brought up from the engine-room. The battery stationed on the hill did not fire a single shot. Obviously, we were not being watched and probably there was no one there to watch us. We were saved.

An easy word to write, 'saved'. Cigarettes were lighted. The charred remains of one of our improvised gunboats were lying sadly on the shore. We found a few wounded men on the other boats. Only then did we notice that the bow of our torpedo-boat had been neatly pierced by a three-inch shell. It was the hour before dawn. We all felt as if we had been born a second time.

One thing followed another. A flier who had just come down with welcome news was brought to me. A detachment of the

Second army under the command of the Cossack Azin had come right up to Kazan from the north-east. They had captured two armoured cars, had disabled two guns, routed an enemy detachment, and occupied two villages twelve versts away from Kazan. The airman flew back at once with instructions and an appeal. Kazan was being squeezed in the clutch of the pincers.

Our night raid, as we soon learned through our reconnaissance men, had cracked the White resistance. The enemy flotilla had been almost completely destroyed, and the shore batteries had been reduced to silence. The word 'torpedo-boat', on the Volga, had the effect on the Whites that the word 'tank' had on the young Red troops before Petrograd some time later. Rumours were spread about to the effect that the Bolsheviks had Germans fighting with them. The prosperous classes began to flee in hordes from Kazan. The workers' districts lifted their heads again. A revolt broke out in the powder-works. An aggressive spirit became apparent among our troops.

The month at Sviyazhsk was crammed full of exciting episodes. Something happened every day. In this respect the nights quite often were not far behind the days. It was the first time that war had unrolled before me so intimately. This was a small war; on our side there were only about 25,000 to 30,000 men engaged. But the small war differed from a big one only in scale. It was like a living model of a war. That is why its fluctuations and surprises were felt so directly. The small war was a big school.

Meanwhile the situation before Kazan changed beyond recognition. Heterogeneous detachments became regular units, buttressed by worker-communists from Petrograd, Moscow and other places. The regiments stiffened up. Inside the units the commissaries acquired the importance of revolutionary leaders, of direct representatives of the dictatorship. The tribunals demonstrated to everyone that Revolution, when threatened by mortal danger, demands the highest sacrifice. Propaganda, organization, revolutionary example and repression produced the necessary change in a few weeks. A vacillating, unreliable and crumbling mass was transformed into a real army. Our artillery had emphatically established its superiority. Our flotilla controlled the river. Our airmen dominated the air. No longer did I doubt that we would take Kazan.

Suddenly on 1 September, I received a code telegram from Moscow: 'Come at once. Vladimir Ilyich wounded, how dangerously not yet known. Complete order prevails. 31 August 1918. Svyerdlov.' I left at once. The mood of the party circles in Moscow was sullen and dismal, but they were absolutely unshakable. The best expression of this determination was Svyerdlov. The physicians declared that Lenin's life was not in danger and promised an early recovery. I encouraged the party with the prospects of success in the East, and returned at once to Sviyazhsk.

Kazan was taken on 10 September. Two days later Simbirsk was occupied by our First army. This was no surprise to me. The commander of the First army, Tukhachevsky, had promised at the end of August that we would take Simbirsk not later than 12 September. When the town was taken, he sent a telegram. ' Order carried out. Simbirsk taken.' Meanwhile Lenin had been recovering. He sent a jubilant telegram of greetings. Things were improving all along the line.

The Fifth army was now headed by Ivan Nikitich Smirnov. This was vastly important. Smirnov represented the most complete and finished revolutionary type; he had entered the ranks thirty years before, and had neither known nor sought for relief. In the darkest years of the reaction Smirnov went on digging underground passages. When they caved in, he did not lose heart but began all over again. Ivan Nikitich was always a man of duty. In this respect a revolutionary resembles a good soldier, and that is why a revolutionary can become a fine one.

Obeying only the demands of his own nature, Ivan Nikitich was always a model of firmness and bravery, without that cruelty which so often accompanies them. All the finest workers of the army began to take him as their example. 'No one was more respected than Ivan Nikitich,' wrote Larissa Reisner in her description of the siege of Kazan. ' One felt that at the most critical moment he would be the strongest and the bravest.' Smirnov has not a trace of pedantry. He is the most sociable, cheerful, and witty of men. People submit to his authority all the more readily because it is not at all obvious or peremptory, even though quite indisputable. As they grouped themselves about Smirnov, the communists of the Fifth army formed a separate political family which. even today, several years after the liquidation of that Fifth army, plays a part in the life of the country.

'A Fifth-army man', in the lexicon of the Revolution, carries a special meaning; it denotes a true revolutionary, a man of duty and, above all, a scrupulous one. With Ivan Nikitich, the men of the Fifth army, after the termination of the civil war, transferred all their heroism to economics, and almost without exception found themselves in .the ranks of the (left) opposition. Smirnov stood at the head of the military industry, then he held the office of commissary of post and telegraph. Today he is in exile in the Caucasus. In prisons and in Siberia you will find many of his fellow heroes of the Fifth army. But Revolution is a great devourer of men and character! The latest reports have it that even Smirnov has been broken by the struggle and is preaching surrender.

Larissa Reisner, who called Ivan Nikitich 'the conscience of Sviyazhsk', was herself prominent in the Fifth army, as well as in the Revolution as a whole. This fine young woman flashed across the revolutionary sky like a burning meteor, blinding many. With her appearance of an Olympian goddess, she combined a subtle and ironical mind and the courage of a warrior. After the capture of Kazan by the Whites she went into the enemy camp to reconnoitre, disguised as a peasant woman. But her appearance was too extraordinary, and she was arrested.

While she was being cross-examined by a Japanese intelligence officer, she took advantage of an interval to slip through the carelessly guarded door and disappear. After that she engaged in intelligence work. Later she sailed on war-boats and took part in battles. Her sketches about the civil war are literature. With equal gusto she would write about the Ural industries and the rising of the workers in the Ruhr. She was anxious to know and to see all and to take part in everything.

In a few brief years she became a writer of the first rank. But after coming unscathed through fire and water this Pallas of the Revolution suddenly burned up with typhus in the peaceful surroundings of Moscow, before she was even thirty.

One good worker joined another. Under fire men learned in a week. The army was taking shape magnificently. The lowest ebb of the Revolution – the moment of the fall of Kazan – was now behind us. Along with this a tremendous change was taking place in the peasantry. The Whites were teaching the muzhiks their political ABCs. During the ensuing seven months the Red Army cleared a territory of nearly a million square kilometres, with a population of forty millions. The Revolution was again advancing. When they fled from Kazan, the Whites carried away with them the gold reserves of the republic, which had been stored there since the February offensive of General Hoffmann. We recaptured them considerably later, and with them Admiral Kolchak.

When I was at last able to take my eyes from Sviyazhsk, I observed that certain changes had taken place in Europe. The German army was in a hopeless position.

The train of the Chairman of the Military Revolutionary Council

The Train

Now it is time to speak of 'The Train' (of the Predrevoyenso-viet*). During the most strenuous years of the Revolution my own personal life was bound up inseparably with the life of that train. The train, on the other hand, was inseparably bound up with the life of the Red Army. The train linked the front with the base, solved urgent problems on the spot, educated, appealed, supplied, rewarded, and punished.

An army cannot be built without reprisals. Masses of men cannot be led to death unless the army command has the death penalty in its arsenal. So long as those malicious tailless apes that are so proud of their technical achievements – the animals that we call men – will build armies and wage wars, the command will always be obliged to place the soldiers between the possible death in the front and the inevitable one in the rear.

And yet armies are not built on fear. The Tsar's army fell to pieces not because of any lack of reprisals. In his attempt to .

save it by restoring the death penalty Kerensky only finished it. Upon the ashes of the great war the Bolsheviks created a new army. These facts demand no explanation for anyone who has even the slightest knowledge of the language of history. The strongest cement in the new army was the ideas of the October Revolution, and the train supplied the front with this cement.

In the provinces of Kaluga, Voronezh, and Ryazan tens of thousands of young peasants had failed to answer the first recruiting summons by the Soviets. The war was going on far from their provinces, the registration of conscripts was inefficient, and consequently the draft to service was not taken seriously.

Those who failed to present themselves were known as deserters. It became necessary to launch a strong campaign against these absentees. The war commissariat of Ryazan succeeded in gathering in some fifteen thousand of such deserters. While passing through Ryazan I decided to take a look at them. Some of our men tried to dissuade me. 'Something might happen,' they warned me. But everything went off beautifully. The men were called out of their barracks. 'Comrade-deserters – come to the meeting. Comrade Trotsky has come to speak to you.' They ran out excited, boisterous, as curious as schoolboys. I had imagined them much worse, and they had imagined me as more terrible. In a few minutes I was surrounded by a huge crowd of unbridled, utterly undisciplined, but not at all hostile men.

The 'comrade-deserters' were looking at me with such curiosity that it seemed as if their eyes would pop out of their heads. I climbed on a table there in the yard and spoke to them for about an hour and a half. It was a most responsive audience. I tried to raise them in their own eyes; concluding, I asked them to lift their hands in token of their loyalty to the Revolution. The new ideas infected them before my very eyes. They were genuinely enthusiastic; they followed me to the automobile, devoured me with their eyes, not fearfully, as before, but rapturously, and shouted at the tops of their voices. They would hardly let me go. I learned afterwards, with some pride, that one of the best ways to educate them was to remind them: 'What did you promise Comrade Trotsky?' Later on, regiments of Ryazan 'deserters' fought well at the fronts.

Every regiment, every company, comprises men of different qualities. The intelligent and self-sacrificing are in the minority. At the opposite pole is an insignificant number of the completely demoralized, the skulkers, and the consciously hostile. Between these two minorities is a large middle group, the undecided, the vacillating. And when the better elements have been lost in fighting or shoved aside, and the skulkers and enemies gain the upper hand, the unit goes to pieces. In such cases the large middle group do not know whom to follow and, in the moment of danger, succumb to panic.

On 24 February 1919, I said to the young commanders gathered in the Hall of Columns in Moscow: ' Give me three thousand deserters, call them a regiment; I will give them a fighting commander, a good commissary, fit officers for battalions, companies and platoons – and these three thousand deserters in the course of four weeks in our revolutionary country will produce a splendid regiment . . . During the last few weeks,' I added, 'we tested this again by experience in the Narva and Pskov sections of the front, where we succeeded in making fine fighting units out of a few scattered fragments.'

For two and a half years, except for comparatively short intervals, I lived in a railway-coach that had formerly been used by one of the ministers of communication. The car was well fitted out from the point of view of ministerial comfort, but it was scarcely adapted to work. There I received those who brought reports, held conferences with local military and civil authorities, studied telegraphic dispatches, dictated orders and articles. From it I made long trips along the front in automobiles with my co-workers. In my spare time I dictated my book against Kautsky, and various other works. In those years I accustomed myself, seemingly forever, to writing and thinking to the accompaniment of Pullman wheels and springs.

My train was hurriedly organized in Moscow on the night of 7 August 1918. In the morning I left in it for Sviyazhsk, bound for the Czecho-Slovak front. The train was continually being reorganized and improved upon, and extended in its functions. As early as 1918 it had already become a flying apparatus of administration.

Its sections included a secretariat, a printing press, a telegraph station, a radio station, an electric-power station, a library, a garage, and a bath. The train was so heavy that it needed two engines; later it was divided into two trains. When we had to stop for some time at some one section of the front, one of the engines would do service as courier and the other was always under steam. The front was shifting constantly and one could take no chances.

I haven't the history of the train at hand. It is buried in the archives of the war department. At one time it was painstakingly worked over by my young assistants. The diagram of the train's movements prepared for the civil-war exhibition used to attract a great many visitors, as the newspapers reported at the time. Later it was put in the civil-war museum. Today it must be hidden away with hundreds and thousands of other exhibits, such as placards, proclamations, orders, flags, photographs, films, books and speeches reflecting the most important moments of the civil war and connected in some way or other with my part in it.

During the years of 1922 to 1924, that is, before repressions were begun against the opposition, the military publishing house managed to bring out five volumes of my works relating to the army and the civil war. The history of the train is not dealt with in these volumes. I can only partially reconstruct the orbit of the train's movements from the place names under the leading articles in the train newspaper, En Route – Samara, Chelyabinsk, Vyatka, Petrograd, Balashov, Smolensk, Samara again, Rostov-on-Don, Novocherkassk, Kiev, Zhitomir, and so on, without end.

I haven't even the exact figures of the total distance covered by the train during the civil war. One of the notes to my military books mentions thirty-six trips, with a total run of over 105,000 kilometres. One of my former fellow travellers writes that he reckons from memory that in three years we circled the earth five and a half times – he gives, that is, a figure twice as large as the one mentioned above. This does not include thousands of kilometres done by automobile from the railway line into the heart of the front lines.

Since the train always went to the most critical points, the diagram of its journeyings gives a fairly exact and comprehensive picture of the relative importance of the different fronts. The greatest number of trips was in 1920, the last year of the war. My trips to the southern front were especially frequent, because all during that period it was the most stubborn, dangerous and extended of all the fronts.

What was the train of the Chairman of the Military Revolutionary Council seeking on the civil-war fronts? The general answer is obvious: it was seeking victory. But what did it give the fronts? What methods did it follow? What were the immediate objects of its endless runs from one end of the country to the other? They were not mere trips of inspection. No, the work of the train was all bound up with the building-up of the army, with its education, its administration, and its supply. We were constructing an army all over again and under fire at that.

This was true not only at Sviyazhsk, where the train recorded its first month, but on all the fronts. Out of bands of irregulars, of refugees escaping from the Whites, of peasants mobilized in the neighbouring districts, of detachments of workers sent by the industrial centres, of groups of communists and trade-unionists – out of these we formed at the front companies, battalions, new regiments, and sometimes even entire divisions. Even after defeats and retreats the flabby, panicky mob would be transformed in two or three weeks into an efficient fighting force. What was needed for this? At once much and little.

It needed good commanders, a few dozen experienced fighters, a dozen or so of communists ready to make any sacrifice, boots for the barefooted, a bath-house, an energetic propaganda campaign, food, underwear, tobacco and matches. The train took care of all this. We always had in reserve a few zealous communists to fill in the breaches, a hundred or so of good fighting men, a small stock of boots, leather jackets, medicaments, machine-guns, field-glasses, maps, watches and all sorts of gifts. Of course, the actual material resources of the train were slight in comparison with the needs of the army, but they were constantly being replenished.

But – what is even more important – tens and hundreds of times they played the part of the shovelful of coal that is necessary at a particular moment to keep the fire from going out. A telegraph station was in operation on the train. We made our connections with Moscow by direct wire, and my deputy there, Sklyansky, took down my demands for supplies urgently needed for the army, sometimes for a single division or even for a regiment. They were delivered with a dispatch that would have been absolutely impossible without my intervention.

Of course, this is not exactly a proper way of doing things – a pedant would tell us that in the supply service, as in military departments in general, the most important thing is system. That is absolutely true. I am myself rather inclined to err on the side of pedantry. But the point is that we did not want to perish before we could build up a smoothly running system. That is why, especially in that early period, we had to substitute improvisations for a system – so that later on we might develop a system on their foundations.

On all of my trips I was accompanied by the chief workers in all the principal departments of the army, especially in those connected with the supply service. We had inherited, from the old army, supply service officers who tried to work in the old way or in even worse fashion, for the conditions became infinitely more difficult. On these trips many of the old specialists had to learn new ways, and new ones received their training in live experience.

After making the round of a division and ascertaining its needs on the spot I would hold a conference in the staff-car or the dining-car, inviting as many representatives as possible, including those from the lower commanding force and from the ranks, as well as from the local party organizations, the Soviet administration, and the trades-unions. In this way I got a picture of the situation that was neither false nor highly coloured. These conferences always had immediate practical results. No matter how poor the organs of the local administration might be they always managed to squeeze a little tighter and cut down some of their own needs to contribute something to the army.

The most important sacrifices came from institutions. A new group of communists would be drawn from the institutions and put immediately into an unreliable regiment. Stuff would be found for shirts and for wrappings for the feet, leather for new soles, and an extra hundredweight of fat. But, of course, the local sources were not enough. After the conference I would send orders to Moscow by direct wire, estimating our needs according to the resources of the centre, and, as a result, the division would get what it desperately needed, and that in good time.

The commanders and commissaries of the front learned from their experience on the train to approach their own work – whether they were commanding, educating, supplying or administering justice – not from above, from the standpoint of the pinnacle of the staff, but from below, from the standpoint of the company or platoon, of the young and inexperienced new recruit.

Gradually, more or less efficient machinery for a centralized supply service for the front and the armies was established. But, alone, it did not and could not satisfy all needs. Even the most ideal organization will occasionally miss fire during a war, and especially during a war of manoeuvres based entirely on movement – sometimes (alas!) in quite unforeseen directions. And one must not forget that we fought without supplies. As early as 1919 there was nothing left in the central depots. Shirts were sent to the front direct from the workshop. But the supply of rifles and cartridges was most difficult of all.

The Tula munition factories worked for the needs of the current day. Not a carload of cartridges could be sent anywhere without the special authorization of the Commander-in-Chief. The supply of munitions was always as taut as a string. Sometimes the string would break and then we lost men and territory.

Without constant changes and improvisations, the war would have been utterly impossible for us. The train initiated these, and at the same time regulated them. If we gave an impulse of initiative to the front and its immediate rear, we took care to direct it into the channels of the general system. I do not want to say that we always succeeded in this. But, as the civil war has demonstrated, we did achieve the principal thing – victory. The trips to the sections of the front where often the treason of the commanding officers had created catastrophes were especially important. On 23 August 1918 during the most critical period before Kazan I received a coded telegram from Lenin and Svyerdlov:

Sviyazhsk Trotsky. Treason on the Saratov front, though discovered in time, has yet produced very dangerous wavering. We consider your going there at once absolutely necessary, for your appearance at the front has an effect on soldiers and the entire army. Let us together arrange for your visits to other fronts Reply stating date of your departure, all by code, 22 August 1918. Lenin. Svyerdlov.

I thought it quite impossible to leave Sviyazhsk, as the departure of the train would have shaken the Kazan front, which was having a difficult enough time as it was. Kazan was in all respects more important than Saratov. Lenin and Svyerdlov themselves soon agreed with me on this. I went to Saratov only after the recapture of Kazan. But telegrams like this reached the train at all stages of its travel. Kiev and Vyatka, Siberia and the Crimea would complain of their difficult positions and would demand, in turn or at the same time, that the train hasten to their rescue.

The war unrolled on the periphery of the country, often in the most remote parts of a front that stretched for eight thousand kilometres. Regiments and divisions were cut off from the rest of the world for months at a time. Very often they had not enough telephone equipment even for their own intercommunication, and would then succumb to hopelessness. The train, for them, was a messenger from other worlds. We always had a stock of telephone apparatus and wires.

A wireless aerial had been arranged over a particular car in our train, so that we could receive radio messages from the Eiffel Tower, from Nauen, and from other stations, thirteen in all, with Moscow, of course, foremost. The train was always informed of what was going on in the rest of the world. The more important telegraphic reports were published in the train newspaper, and given passing comment in articles, leaflets and orders. Kapp's raid, conspiracies at home, the English elections, the progress of grain collections, and feats of the Italian Fascismo were interpreted while the footprints of events were still warm, and were linked up with the fates of the Astrakhan or Archangel fronts.

These articles were simultaneously transmitted to Moscow by direct wire, and radioed from there to the press of the entire country. The arrival of the train put the most isolated unit in touch with the whole army, and brought it into the life not only of the country, but of the entire world. Alarmist rumours and doubts were dispelled, and the spirit of the men grew firm. This change of morale would last for several weeks, sometimes until the next visit of the train. In the intervals, members of the Military-Revolutionary Council of the front or the army would make trips similar in character, but on a smaller scale.

All my work in the train, literary and otherwise, would have been impossible without my assisting stenographers, Glazman and Syermuks, and the younger assistant, Nechayev. They worked all day and all night in the moving train, which, disregarding all rules of safety in the fever of war, would rush over shaken ties at a speed of seventy or more kilometres an hour, so that the map that hung from the ceiling of the car would rock like a swing. I would watch in wondering gratitude the movements of the hand that, despite the incessant jerking and shaking, could inscribe the finely shaped symbols so clearly. When I was handed the typed script half an hour later, no corrections were necessary. This was not ordinary work; it took on a character of heroic sacrifice. Afterwards, Glazman and Syermuks paid dearly for their sacrifices in the service of the Revolution. Glazman was driven to suicide by the Stalinists, and Syermuks has been shut away in the wilds of Siberia.

Part of the train was a huge garage holding several automobiles and a gasoline tank. This made it possible for us to travel away from the railway line for several hundred versts. A squad of picked sharpshooters and machine-gunners, amounting to from twenty to thirty men, occupied the trucks and light cars. A couple of hand machine-guns had also been placed in my car. A war of movement is full of surprises. On the steppes we always ran the risk of running into some Cossack band.

Automobiles with machine-guns insured one against this, at least when the steppe had not been transformed into a sea of mud. Once, during the autumn of 1919, in the province of Voronezh, we could move at a speed of only three kilometres an hour. The automobiles sank deep into the black, rain-soaked earth. Thirty men had to keep jumping off their cars to push them along. And once, when we were fording a river, we got stuck in midstream.

In a rage I blamed everything on the low-built machine which my excellent chauffeur, an Estonian named Puvi, considered the very best machine in the world. He turned round to me, and raising his hand to his cap, said in broken Russian: ' I beg to state that the engineers never foresaw that we should have to sail on water.'

In spite of the difficulty of the moment I felt like embracing him for the cold aptness of his irony.

The train was not only a military-administrative and political institution, but a fighting institution as well. In many of its features it was more like an armoured train than a staff headquarters on wheels. In fact it was armoured, or at least its engines and machine-gun cars were. All the crew could handle arms. They all wore leather uniforms, which always make men look heavily imposing. On the left arm, just below the shoulder, each wore a large metal badge, carefully cast at the mint, which had acquired great popularity in the army.

The cars were connected by telephone and by a system of signals. To keep the men on the alert while we were travelling, there were frequent alarms, both by day and by night. Armed detachments would be put off the train as 'landing parties'. The appearance of a leather-coated detachment in a dangerous place invariably had an overwhelming effect. When they were aware of the presence of the train just a few kilometres behind the firing-line, even the most nervous units, their commanding officers especially, would summon up all their strength, In the unstable poise of a scale only a small weight is enough to decide. The role of that weight was played by the train and its detachments a great many times during its two-and-a-half years of travel.

When we took the returned 'landing party' aboard, we usually found someone missing. Altogether the train lost about fifteen men in killed and wounded, not counting the ones who joined the units in the field and disappeared from our view. For instance, a squad was made up from our train crew for the model armoured train named for Lenin; another joined the troops in the field before Petrograd. For its share in the battles against Yudenich the train as a whole was decorated with the order of the Red Flag.

Sometimes the train was cut off and shelled or bombed from the air. No wonder it was surrounded by a legend woven of victories both real and imagined. Time and again the commander of a division, of a brigade, or even of a regiment would ask me to stay at his staff headquarters for an extra half-hour,   just whiling away the time, or to drive with him by automobile or on horseback to some distant sector, or even to send a few men from the train there with supplies and gifts, so that the news of the train's arrival might be spread far and wide. 'This will be as good as a division in reserve,' commanders would say.

The news of the arrival of the train would reach the enemy lines as well. There people imagined a mysterious train infinitely more awful than it really was. But that only served to increase its influence on morale. The train earned the hatred of its enemies and was proud of it. More than once the Socialist-Revolutionists made plans to wreck it. At the trial of the Socialist-Revolutionists the story was told in detail by Semyonov, who organized the assassination of Volodarsky and the attempt on Lenin's life and who also took part in the preparations to wreck the train. As a matter of fact, such an enterprise presented no great difficulty, except that by that time the Socialist-Revolutionists, weakened politically, had lost faith in themselves and no longer had much influence with the younger generation.

On one of our trips south the train was wrecked at the station of Gorky. In the middle of the night I was suddenly jerked out of bed, and was seized by that creepy feeling one has during an earthquake of the ground slipping away under one's feet with no firm support anywhere. Still half-asleep, I clutched the sides of the bed. The familiar rumbling had stopped at once; the car had turned on its edge and stood stock-still. In the silence of the night, a single, pitiful voice was the only thing to be heard. The heavy car-doors were so bent that they could even be opened, and I could not get out. No one appeared, which alarmed me. Was it the enemy? With a revolver in my hand I jumped out of the window and ran into a man with a lantern. It was the commander of the train, unable to get to me,

The car was standing on a slope, with three wheels buried deep in the embankment, and the other three rising high above the rails. The rear and front of the car had crumpled. The front grating had pinned down a sentry, and it was his pitiful little voice, like the crying of a child, that I had heard in the darkness. It was no easy matter to release him from the grating covering him so tightly. To everyone's surprise, he got off with nothing but bruises and a scare.

In all, eight cars were destroyed. The restaurant car, which was used as the club for the train, was a heap of polished splinters. A number of men had been reading or playing chess while they waited for their turn to go on duty, but they had left the club at midnight, ten minutes before the accident. The trucks with books, equipment and gifts for the front were all badly damaged as well. None of the men was seriously hurt.

The accident was due to faulty switching, whether because of negligence or deliberate action we never found out. Fortunately for us the train was passing a station at the time, running at a speed of only thirty kilometres. The train crew performed many other tasks besides their special duties. They lent their help in time of famine, during epidemics of disease, in propaganda campaigns, and at international congresses. The train was the honorary head of a rural district and of several children's homes. Its communist local published its own paper, *On Guard*. Many an incident of adventure and battle is recorded in its pages, but unfortunately this, like many other records, is not in my present travelling archives.

When I was leaving to prepare an offensive against Wrangel, who had entrenched himself in the Crimea, I wrote in the train newspaper *En Route* on 27 October 1920:

> Our train is again bound for the front. The fighting men
> of our train were before the walls of Kazan in the grave
> weeks of 1918, when we were fighting for the control of
> the Volga. That fight ended long ago. Today the Soviet
> power is approaching the Pacific Ocean. The fighting
> men of our train fought gallantly before the walls of
> Petrograd. Petrograd has been saved and has since been
> visited by many representatives of the world proletariat.
> Our train visited the western front more than once, Today,

a preliminary peace has been signed with Poland. The fighting men of our train were on the steppes of the Don when Krasnov and, later, Denikin advanced against Soviet Russia from the south. The days of Krasnov and Denikin are long since passed. There now is left only the Crimea, which the French government has made its fortress. The White Guard garrison of this French fortress is under the command of a hired German-Russian general, Baron Wrangel. The friendly family of our train is starting on a new campaign. Let this campaign be the last.

The Crimean campaign was actually the last campaign of the civil war. A few months later the train was disbanded. From these pages I send fraternal greetings to all my former comrades in-arms.

Trotsky's Left Opposition. Moscow, 1927. Ivan Smirnov is seated in the front row, second from the left, next to Trotsky (centre). (Source: David King)

✪ BIOGRAPHICAL SKETCHES*

Ivan Nikitovich Smirnov (1881- 1936)

I was born into a peasant family in Ryazan province. When I was roughly two, our family was ruined by a fire. My father went to work in Moscow and died there a year later. Then my mother went to Moscow to work as a domestic servant. I was eight years old before I was taken to join her there. In Moscow I went to a municipal school and then found work on the railways and in a factory. In 1898 I first became acquainted with Socialist Democratic literature and began to meet a few students who engaged in propaganda. Whilst at the factory I came across the two or three workers who remained from the organisation smashed in 1896. We formed a workers' self-education circle with roughly fifteen members, of whom three to my knowledge have remained in the Party.

In 1899 I was arrested for the first time, held for roughly two years and then deported to Irkutsk province for five years. After

---

*From *Makers of the Russian Revolution*, Georges Haupt, George Allen & Unwin, 1974

eight months, however, I escaped. The CC Party Bureau, which at that time was in Pskov, sent me to work in Tver province. The local committee directed me to Vyshny Volochek where there were roughly ten thousand workers with whom it had no contact, and I found a job as a labourer at the Proskuryakov tannery. I worked there for nearly six months. I managed to establish a following in the Prokhorov and Ryabushinsky works, both large factories, but just when the work was beginning to go well, I was denounced by Sladkov, a worker dismissed from the Ryabushinsky factory. I was arrested, and the man sent by the Tver Committee to take my place was also quickly caught. Nevertheless, on May Day 1904, proclamations were distributed in Vyshny Volochek and a small strike took place.

I spent two years in prison. Then I was tried for spreading propaganda (this was already 1905), and, moreover, our case was heard in Moscow two days after the massacre in St Petersburg on 9 January.* I was sentenced to one year in a fortress, but the court took into account my preliminary detention and set me free. Since my administrative exile was still not completed, the police made a search for me.

At this time, I began to work for the Moscow Committee as organiser for the Lefortovo district. In March I was rearrested. It was intended that I should go back to exile in Irkutsk province, but the Trans-Siberian railway was fully occupied with ferrying

---

* On 22 January 1905, a Sunday, a demonstration of workers in St Petersburg, led by the priest Father Gapon (later found to have been a police spy) marched to the Winter Palace in St Petersburg. They carried a petition in which they set out their grievances and appealed to the Tsar, Nicholas II, for improvements to their lot. Among their complaints were that: 'Despotism and arbitrariness are suffocating us, we are gasping for breath'. The demonstrators included men, women and children carrying church banners and portraits of the Tsar. When they reached Palace Square, their progress was halted by soldiers of the Imperial Guard who opened fire and hacked down protestors with sabres. It has been estimated that 1,000 were killed, another 5,000 wounded and up to 7,000 arrested. The massacre, which became known as Bloody Sunday, was the trigger for the 1905 revolution in Russia. Nicholas II was renamed the Bloody Tsar.

troops for the Russo-Japanese war, and I was sent instead to Vologda province. On the way I contracted typhus and arrived in exile three months before the strike of October 1905. The amnesty that followed this strike freed me from the rest of my sentence. I returned to Moscow and resumed my activities. During the armed insurrection I was organiser for the Blagusha sub-district in the Lefortovo district. But as I heavily compromised myself during these days, I had to leave Blagusha once the rising had been crushed, and I moved to the railway district.

I remained in Moscow until 1909 when I was again accused of organising the distribution of banned literature – at this time I was working in the Moscow Committee's bookshop. The charge could not be substantiated with evidence, however, and it was dismissed. In 1909 I was banished from Moscow and went to St Petersburg. I worked for the Committee there as organiser for the Peterburgskaya Storona district. In June 1910 I was betrayed by the agent provocateur Bryandinsky and after a short spell in custody I was deported to the area of Narym where I remained for eighteen months. Then I learnt that I might be moved from Narym to the Turukhansk region. So I escaped with a group of comrades who were all threatened with the same fate. After my escape I worked in Rostov and Kharkov.

In 1913 I managed to unite the two separate groups of Bolsheviks and Mensheviks in Kharkov, and I was active there until July. Then the organisation was penetrated by two skilful Provocateurs (Sigaev and Rudov), and I was arrested. I was sent to Narym, and moreover was sentenced to six months imprisonment for a trivial matter (a demonstration). After I had served this sentence, I was mistakenly released at the prison gates and I escaped to Krasnoyarsk. When I had received good identity papers, I returned to Moscow.

There, at the beginning of the war, a group of comrades and I attempted to resurrect the local organisation, but after six months I was arrested on information from the agent provocateur Poskrebukhin, and deported back to Narym. The case could not be brought to trial for lack of compromising documents.

I remained in Narym until 1916 when I was pressed into the Tsarist army. The exiles who were called up discussed whether they ought to obey the call or escape, although the latter would have been very difficult. They decided to join, but with the aim of agitating against the war. In Narym a committee was chosen for our future military organisation and I was included in it. Immediately on arrival in Tomsk, we contacted the local organisation. With money received from Moscow, we equipped an underground printing-press and set to work. Our military organisation had very great success and, as far as I know, it was the only one existing at that time. It involved up to two hundred soldiers in Tomsk and a large number in Novonikolaevsk. Proclamations were distributed throughout Siberia. A provocateur, Tsvetkov, joined the committee and, as was later revealed during the February Revolution he was awaiting a suitable moment for betrayal, but events forestalled him.

The military union lost only one comrade, Nakhanovich, who worked on the printing press and subsequently perished in Kolchak's jail. Our union played a very important role in the February uprising. During it I was a member of the Executive Committee of Soldiers' Deputies. In August I left for Moscow where, on the suggestion of the local committee and the Bureau of the Central Region, I founded the Party publication, *Volna* (*The Agitator*).

At the outbreak of Civil War, the CC sent me to Kazan. There I was appointed member of the RVS (Revolutionary Military Soviet), on the Eastern Front. In December 1919 I changed from military work to conspiratorial activity in the enemy's rear, for which I joined the newly formed CC Siberian Bureau. Subsequently, in the aftermath of the defeat of the Fifth Army, I was appointed to its RVS, combining this with my other work. After the defeat of Kolchak, I was made Chairman of the Siberian Revolutionary Committee. In 1921, I was transferred to Party work in Petrograd where I was Secretary of the local committee and the North-Western Regional Bureau of the CC. After six months in these positions, I worked for a year in the VSNKh (Supreme Soviet of the National Economy) where I was in charge of the armaments industry. Then I was appointed to the People's Commissariat for Trade and Industry.

In all I spent roughly six years in prison and never completed a sentence of banishment, although I did spend roughly four years in exile.'

First and foremost, Ivan Smirnov was the man of the Fifth Army, the army which repulsed Kolchak and the Czech Legion on the Eastern Front, liberated Siberia and managed to absorb an enormous army of peasant partisans. He was a member of the Eastern Front RVS then a member of the Fifth Army RVS and President of the Siberian Bureau, which operated clandestinely in Siberia under Kolchak's occupation. Subsequently, in 1921 and 1922, Smirnov ran the war industries. Elected to alternate membership of the Central Committee in March 1919, and to full membership in April 1920, he joined Trotsky's platform on the trade union question and was only re-elected to alternate membership in March 1921. In 1922, he lost his position on the Central Committee altogether and for good.

Later on, a member of the Marxist-Leninist Institute recalled that at a preparatory meeting before the twelfth Congress, Ivan Smirnov's name was put to Lenin for the secretaryship of the Party. Smirnov had just lost the secretaryship of the organisation (replaced by Uglanov) and had been transferred to Siberia. Lenin, according to the story, hesitated before replying, 'Ivan Smirnov is essential in Siberia.'

He was signatory to the 'Declaration of the 46', Commissar for Posts from 1923 to 1927, leader of the United Opposition, and was expelled from the Party in 1927 before being exiled to Siberia. Smirnov was scarcely an 'ideologist', but he was greedy for action. He rallied to Stalin at the end of the summer of 1929 : he could not watch 'the building of socialism' without having a part in it, even if he rejected some of its methods. But disillusionment was quick to come.

In 1932 he entrusted Leon Sedov with an unsigned article for the *Byulletin Oppozitsiy*. A few months later, early in 1933, he was arrested by the police in connection with the Ryutin affair. In August 1936, he was among the defendants at the first Moscow Trial, and 'confessed' to having participated in the assassination of Kirov, even though he was in prison at the time. Sentenced to death like the other fifteen defendants, he refused to sign his appeal for pardon out of anger at having been led to make an incriminating confession.

Larissa Reisner wrote of him: 'Outside any rank or right, Smirnov was the incarnation of the revolutionary ethic, he was the highest moral criterion of the communist consciousness at Sviyazhsk. Comrade Smirnov's exceptional purity and probity imposed themselves even on the mass of non-party soldiers and on the communists who had not known him before.' He had a gentle sense of humour which pierced through his few written works, and even more in an anecdote told by Victor Serge. Dismissed from the People's Commissariat for Posts in 1927, Smirnov commented, 'It would do us all good to go back to the ranks for a while' – and being penniless went to the Labour Exchange where he registered as an unemployed precision machinist. On his card under the heading 'Last job held' he wrote 'People's Commissar for Posts'. Serge adds, 'For the younger generation he incarnated the idealism of his

Party, without rhetoric or embroidery.' Smirnov's name is still omitted from republications of contemporary texts. He has not yet been allowed back onto the General Staff or the RVS of the Fifth Army, which, without Rosengolts or Smirnov, look rather skeletal. (Biographical note compiled by Jean-Jacques Marie, in Biographies of Bolshevik Leaders, *Makers of the Russian Revolution*).

Nikolay Grigorevich Markin (1893–1918)

Nikolay Markin, whose exploits deserve an entire chapter in Larissa Reisner's dispatches from the frontline, was a close confidant of Trotsky and organiser of the Volga Military Flotilla. Markin was born to a peasant family in the Russian village of Syroınyas, now named Markino in his honour. He was first arrested for his political activity in 1910, aged 17, while working in a printshop. He spent eight months in prison.

In 1914, at the age of 21, he was drafted into the Baltic Fleet, where he became a non-commissioned officer at the Kronstadt naval base. He joined the RSDLP (Russian Social Democratic Labour Party) in 1916 and was an active participant in the February Revolution of 1917.

He was a member of the Kronstadt Committee of the RSDLP, the Kronstadt Soviet and representative of the sailors of the Baltic Fleet on the Petrograd Soviet. He was one of the organizers of the 1st Baltic Sailors' Congress and, from April 1917, he served in the detachment guarding Lenin. He also took part in the October Revolution. When Trotsky was appointed commissioner of foreign affairs he looked to Markin for assistance when he found that: '…it seemed impossible to get down to business' because 'everyone was involved in sabotage. The cupboards were locked. There were no keys.' Markin was appointed secretary and then controller of the

Foreign Affairs Department and, according to Trotsky, in effect became the unacknowleged foreign minister. In early June 1918, Markin was sent to Nizhny Novgorod with the task of creating the Volga Military Flotilla.

In September 1918, during the battles for Kazan, Markin led the landing operation. Under the cover of artillery fire, the four torpedo boats of the Volga flotilla overcame the White artillery batteries with machine gun fire and mounted an amphibious attack on the naval base. On the night of September 9-10, 1918, the destroyers *Prytky* (*Lively*) and *Retive* (*Ardent*) led a larger amphibious assault, with a combined battalion of soldiers and sailors. The following month, on 1 October 1918, the gunboat *Vanya-Communist* was ambushed during reconnaissance along the River Kama. The ship was sunk and Markin went down with it while he provided covering fire for the other crew members from the machine gun mounted on the deck.

In his obituary, Trotsky wrote: 'Nikolai Markin was killed in action on his steamer *Communist*. Among our many losses it is one of the most severe. He was relatively little known in the party and in soviet organizations, because he was not a journalist or speaker; but his deeds were brighter and more expressive than any words. I knew him intimately and I testify that Markin was one of the best in our ranks. I can't believe he's not with us anymore. Goodbye, faithful good friend Markin!

In 1968, the Russian State Post Office issued a commemorative stamp in honour of Markin as a hero of the Civil War. A monument to the heroes of the Volga Military Flotilla was installed in Markin Square in Nizhny Novgorod and Markin's birthplace was renamed Markino in 1960. A monument was also erected on the Volga riverbank where Markin was killed and, in 1939, a street in Leningrad (formerly Olonetska Street) was renamed Markin Street.

Nestor Ivanovich Makhno (1888–1934)

Makhno was an anarcho-communist and commander of the Revolutionary Insurrectionary Army of the Ukraine. With its roots among the peasantry, his army became known as the *Mahnovshchina*, or Makhno movement. It came to exert a strong influence over large areas of southern Ukraine during the the Civil War.

Makhno was aggressively opposed to all factions that sought to impose their authority over southern Ukraine. He fought the forces of the Ukrainian National Republic, the Central Powers of Germany and Austro-Hungary, the Cossack Hetmanate State, the White Army, the Bolshevik Red Army and other smaller forces led by various Ukrainian atamans.

He is also credited as the inventor of the *tachanka* – a horse-drawn carriage mounted with a heavy machine gun. Makhno and his supporters attempted to reorganize social and economic life along anarchist lines, including the establishment of communes on former landed estates, the requisition and egalitarian redistribution of land to the peasants, and the organization of free elections to local soviets, or councils, and regional congresses.

Although Makhno considered the Bolsheviks a threat to the development of an anarchist Free Territory within Ukraine, he entered into formal military alliances with the Red Army twice in order to defeat the Whites. In the aftermath of the White Army's defeat in Crimea in November 1920, the Bolsheviks initiated a military campaign against Makhno. After an extended period of open resistance, Makhno fled across the Romanian border in August 1921. In exile, Makhno settled in Paris and wrote numerous memoirs and articles for radical journals. Makhno died in 1934 in Paris, of a TB-related illness, at the age of 45.

Vasily Ivanovich Shorin (1870-1938)

Shorin was a company commander in the Tsarist army before joining the Red Army in 1917. He commanded several military units of the Red Army during the Civil War.

He graduated from the Kazan infantry school of the Junkers in 1892. In the Russo-Japanese War of 1904-1905 he commanded a company, and a battalion at the start of World War I. By June 1916, he was Colonel of the 333rd Infantry Glazovsky Regiment.

After the October Revolution, he took the side of the Soviet government. He was elected by the soldiers as commander of the 26th Infantry Division and headed that division during the retaking of Kazan – he is mentioned more than once in Larissa Reisner's account. In September 1918, he was appointed commander of the Second Army of the Eastern Front.

Shorin successfully reorganized the army during the spring offensive of Admiral Kolchak's troops. In 1920 he was a member of the Siberian Revolutionary Committee. From May 1920 to January 1921 he was an assistant to the Commander-in-Chief of the Armed Forces of the Far Eastern Republic, led the suppression of anti-Soviet uprisings and the struggle with the troops of Baron Ungern Von Sternberg.

From 1923 to 1925, Shorin was deputy commander of the troops of the Leningrad Military District. He was arrested in 1938, under Stalin's regime, accused of anti-Soviet agitation. According to some reports he was shot, according to other sources he died in prison before trial. He is buried on the Bogoslovskoe Cemetery in St Petersburg.

Nikolay Stepanovich Gumilyev (1886-1921)

Nikolay Gumilyev was born on 15 April 1886, in Kronstadt, the son of a naval doctor and the grandson of an admiral, L. I. Lvov, on his mother's side. He became an influential Russian poet, literary critic, traveler, and military officer. He co-founded the Acmeist movement in poetry and was married to the doyenne of Russian poetry, Anna Akhmatova. Gumilyev married Akhmatova on 25 April, 1910.

When his family moved to Tbilisi, Georgia, in 1900, because of his brother Dmitry's tuberculosis, Gumilyev found the city a hotbed of revolutionary activity and as a boy of fourteen, he was drawn into politics for the first and last time. According to Anna Akhmatova's biographer, Roberta Reeder, Gumilyov read Marx and agitated among the local population, but when his family moved again, to Tsarskoye Selo in 1903, Gumilyev's reading habits changed, and he turned from politics to philosophy and French Symbolism: 'His love for the French Symbolists was shared by Akhmatova, but his interest in Nietzsche marks an important difference between them. By this time Nietzsche had become a powerful influence among Russian intellectuals, proving an attractive figure to those aesthetes who rebelled against the social activism of their parents' generation. They attacked charity and altruism as signs of weakness, preferring instead individualism, ego, and will.

'One of the reasons why Nietzsche's ideas were so readily adopted by this generation was that they were concepts derived from ideas already generated by Dostoyevsky's protagonists—men like Raskolnikov—that God is dead, and therefore all is permitted; that the man-god is beyond good and evil; and that beauty will save the world. Dostoyevsky himself attacked such concepts vigorously, but they were found to be attractive to a generation that replaced moral virtue with an aesthetic sensualism.'

An inveterate womaniser, Gumilyev began an affair with Larissa Reisner in 1916. The two met at the Comedian's Halt a cabaret club that had replaced the Stray Dog as the focus of bohemian social life in St Petersburg. It was closed by the police in March 1915 because of wartime censorship. At the time Reisner was a 21-year old student at the Institute of Psychoneurosis.

Her family were so involved in revolutionary activity that her father had got into trouble while occupying a faculty position in Tomsk. The family fled to Berlin and Paris, where they continued to be involved in leftist causes but, when the situation became more stable in Russia after 1907, the family returned, and her father became a professor of law at Petersburg University.

Reisner wrote fiction and poetry and began a journal, *Rudin*, in 1915, that made satirical attacks on tsarist Russia. Reisner liked Gumilyov's poems and even tried to imitate them. They called each other 'Lefi' and 'Gafiz', and wrote to each other while separated by the war. On 8 December, 1916, he wrote to say how much he missed her: 'Everything I know and love, I want to see as if through coloured glass, through your soul, because it has a special colour. I do not believe in the transmigration of souls, but I think that in your former transmigrations you were the kidnapped Helen of Sparta, Angelina of Orlando Furioso, etc. I want to take you away. I wrote you a crazy letter because I love you. I remember your every word, every nuance, every movement, but it's not enough. I want more. Yours, Gafiz. When a friend asked Akhmatova what Reisner was like, Akhmatova replied acidly, 'I don't know—I know the poetry she wrote was totally tasteless. But she was smart enough to stop writing.' Larissa Reisner's last meeting with Gumilyev took place in April 1917.

At the outset of the First World War, Gumilyev enlisted immediately: 'In war he could prove his love for his homeland and…it was also a realisation of his Nietzchean philosophy… war provided a life-threatening situation, which presented him with the opportunity to show his courage.' By contrast,

Akhmatova wrote poems expressing the horrors of war and Reisner was the driving force behind the anti-war journal, *Rudin*.

Gumilyev fought in battles in East Prussia and Macedonia and was awarded two St George crosses for his bravery. During the Russian Revolution, Gumilyev served in the Russian Expeditionary Force in France. Despite advice to the contrary, he then returned to Petrograd and finally divorced Akhmatova in August, 1918. The following year he married Anna Nikolaevna Engelhardt, a noblewoman and daughter of a well-known historian.

In 1920, Gumilyev co-founded the All-Russia Union of Writers. Gumilyev made no secret of his anti-communist views. He went out of his way to make the sign of the cross in public and didn't care to hide his contempt for what he regarded as the semi-literate Bolsheviks. On 3 August, 1921, he was arrested by the Cheka on dubious charges of participation in an alleged monarchist conspiracy. On 24 August, the Petrograd Cheka decreed the execution of sixty-one participants in the case, including Gumilyev. They were shot on 26 August, in the Kovalevsky Forest. Maxim Gorky, his friend and fellow writer, rushed to Moscow and made a last-gasp appeal to Lenin, but was unable to save Gumilyev.

Lev Gumilyev, the only son of Gumilyev and Akhmatova, was arrested later in the purges of the 1930s and spent almost two decades in the Gulag. Although banned in Soviet times, Gumilyev was loved for his adolescent longing for travel and giraffes and hippos. His 'The Tram That Lost Its Way' is considered one of the greatest poems of the 20th century.

When Larissa Reisner died of typhus in February 1926, Akhmatova was deeply affected, In the words of Roberta Reeder: 'In a distant but implicit way, Reisner's life had touched hers through Gumilyev…No one would ever have imagined that I would outlive Larisa!' she said affectionately, and with great sorrow. 'Here's yet another death. How people are dying! She wanted so much to live, she was cheerful, healthy, and beautiful. You remember how relatively calmly I took the news of Yesenin's death, because he wanted to die and was seeking death. This – is something quite different. But Larissa!'

Larissa Mikhailovna Reisner (1895-1926)

The following biographical sketch was written by Jean-Jacques Marie and included in the anthology *Makers of the Russian Revolution.*

Larissa Mikhailovna Reisner, the daughter of the communist professor M. A. Reisner, was born on 1 May 1895 in the Polish Kingdom in Lublin, where her father was lecturer at the Pulawy Agricultural Institute. She spent her childhood in Germany and went to primary school in Berlin and Heidelberg. There she grew up in an atmosphere dominated by her father's connections with émigré Russian revolutionaries and the leaders of German social democracy. These years sowed the seeds of a lifelong attachment to German culture, and a few years spent in Paris with her parents widened the scope of her cultural interests.

She went to school in Russia just after the suppression of the 1905 Revolution, and already at the Gymnasium she displayed her literary abilities and revolutionary temperament. She took to literature at an early age, and a strong formative influence was a friend of her parents, Leonid Andreyev, who guided her through literary history.

He did not, however, greatly influence her ideas, as can be seen from the drama *Atlantis,* which she wrote at the age of seventeen and which was printed by the Shipovnik publishing house in 1913. The theme of this drama was the attempt of a man to save society by personal sacrifice. The sources from which she drew material for the play — including Pellman's *History of Communism* — clearly indicate the nature of her ideas at that time.

From the very beginning of the war she was acutely distressed by the collapse of international social democracy and the Russian intelligentsia's conversion to chauvinism. She fully agreed with her parents' split with Andreyev on these grounds. For Professor Reisner it was unthinkable that one should hold aloof from the anti-war campaign and this impelled him to publish the journal *Rudin*, which both by outspoken articles and brilliant caricatures of the deserters to the patriotic camp represented a graphic protest against the war by an isolated, intellectual, revolutionary group.

The moving spirit behind Rudin was Larissa, who printed in it not only brilliant, well-turned verses, but also a whole series of pungent sketches. At the same time, she shouldered the burden of arguments with the censorship and the raising of funds. When the latter ran out, *Rudin* had to close, and Larissa began to contribute articles to Gorky's *Letopis* (*The Chronicle*).

In 1917, even before the Revolution, she became associated with workers' circles. The February Revolution set her immediately among the opponents of a coalition with the bourgeoisie. A telling pamphlet against Kerensky printed in *Novaya Zhizn* provoked not only a broadside from the bourgeois press but even frightened the editorial board of Gorky's journal. She also became involved in largescale workers' organisations and circles among the Kronstadt sailors.

The October Revolution met with a ready response from her. During the first months she was busy preserving works of art, not in the spirit of a protector of the old against barbarians, but in order that the best of our cultural heritage should be saved to inspire the creators of the new culture.

The outbreak of civil war destroyed all the attractions of this work. She longed for direct combat, and Sviyazhsk, near Kazan, where the Red Army was being forged in its struggle with the Czechs, saw her in the front line with a rifle in her hand, as veterans of this recounted.

Similarly she later participated in the whole campaign of the Volga Flotilla. A veteran of these battles and former Tsarist officer, F. Novitsky, has told of the respect this young revolutionary earned among experienced soldiers by her intrepidity in the most dangerous situations. After the defeat of the Czechs and the of the Volga, it was inconceivable that she should be separated from the Red Navy, and she was named one of the Commissars on its Staff. Her enthusiasm and sensitivity, allied with her imperturbable and clear-headed reasoning, enabled her to win the respect of top-ranking Tsarist officers like Admirals Altvater and Berens who, after joining the Soviets, needed a dynamic person to help them identify with the Revolution.

When our flotilla was again pressed into service against Denikin, Larissa saw action with it from Astrakhan to Enzeli. After the end of the Civil War, she lived in Petrograd and attempted to study at first hand the life of the working masses in a factory. She was driven to the verge of despair by the Kronstadt rebellion and the beginning of NEP and, full of unease about the future of Soviet Russia, she went to Afghanistan as wife of the Soviet Plenipotentiary there, F. F. Raskolnikov.

In Kabul, she did not remain a mere spectator of the diplomatic struggle between the Soviet representatives and British imperialism. She sought the most active involvement by ingratiating herself with the Emir's harem, since it played an influential role in Afghan politics. From the vantage-point of Afghanistan, which was considered an Indian outpost by the British, she was able to make a study of Britain's policy in India and the Indian nationalist movement.

When she returned from Kabul in 1923, she published *The Front* and *Afghanistan*. The Front will always remain one of the most brilliant literary portrayals of the Civil War. It is remarkable for the sensitivity and attention with which the author observes not only the heroes and leaders of the war, but also the masses who were directly responsible for victory.

In October 1923 she went to Germany with a dual goal. Ostensibly she would evoke for the Russian workers the civil war which was in the offing there as a result of the economic chaos and the seizure of the Ruhr by the French. At the same time, in case of a seizure of power in Saxony, she was to serve as liaison officer between the local German social democratic organisation and the Comintern representatives in Dresden.

Events in Saxony, however, did not develop as had been hoped. After the defeat there, life in Berlin became extremely difficult and she helped to ascertain the moods of the people for the Comintern men who lived as a tight, conspiratorial group. She stood in queues of unemployed at labour exchanges and in front of shops; she went to factory assemblies, social democratic meetings, and hospitals; she participated in the first demonstrations we managed to organise despite the dissolution of the Communist Party by the government.

At the first news of the Hamburg rising she hurried there, but it was a short-lived affair and she only arrived after it had been crushed. She collected details of the heroic resistance of the Hamburg proletariat from the families of fugitives, and she found her way into the courtrooms where summary justice was meted out to the vanquished. She had her material checked by outstanding participants in the rising, returned to Russia, and wrote *Hamburg at the Barricades*, which was printed in the first number of the journal *Zhizn*.

It is a unique work of its kind, for neither the Finnish uprising nor Soviet Hungary has produced its like. The German censorship and the imperial court banned the German edition of the book and ordered it to be burnt. An aesthete protested against the ban in the liberal *Frankfurter Zeitung* in view of the book's great artistic merit, but the class-ridden legal system of the German counter-revolution knew what it was doing in destroying the book which preserved the spirit of the Hamburg uprising for the German proletariat.

Hardly had she recovered from the harsh conditions of the conspiratorial life she had had to lead in Hamburg, than she was off to the Urals to study the living conditions of the proletariat there. This trip not only fulfilled a literary goal. She had already had her doubts about NEP and now she set them against real life. In the backbreaking labour of the engineering workers and the masses, and in the work of administrators scattered in settlements throughout the Urals, she found the answer to the question as to whether we are building socialism or capitalism.

She returned full of faith in our future and threw herself into a study of our economic construction. She tore herself away from her books to visit the Donbass and the textile region. Her book *Iron, Coal and Living People* depicts the Russian proletariat at work. From the artistic point of view it is remarkable for the fact that Larissa, who had grown up among the *Acmeists* and had had a very refined style, was now beginning to write more simply and straightforwardly for the sake of the working masses. This was not artificial vulgarisation but the fruit of the greater rapport with the workers which she achieved during her trips as a propagandist with the Moscow garrison.

In 1925, ill with malaria since the Persian expedition, she set out for treatment in Germany, but even illness could not prevent her from contacting the Hamburg proletariat. She slipped away from the malaria hospital to take part in a demonstration by the Hamburg communists, and after recovering slightly she toured Germany, studying the conditions of the working class and the social changes which had resulted from 'stabilisation'.

She not only visited the workers' quarters, the barracks of mass poverty, but also found her way into the Junkers technical laboratory, the Krupp offices, the huge Ullstein newspaper plant and the coal mines in Westphalia. Her book *In the Country of Hindenburg* is not merely a number of artistic sketches, but a masterful, large-scale socio-political canvas painted by someone deeply sympathetic to the struggle of the working class.

As soon as she finished this work, she set about examining material on the Decembrists. Her sketches of Trubetskoy, Kakhovsky and Shteingel evoked warm praise from the best Russian Marxist historian and also represented the peak of her artistic achievement. She never saw these works in print. She contracted typhus at a time when her head was full of plans for a book about the life of the Urals workers at three periods in history: during the Pugachov revolt, under capitalism and then under Soviet power. She also had in mind a large-scale book on the history of the proletarian movement. Her body had been so ravaged by malaria that it was unable to withstand the illness, and on 9 February 1926 she passed away in the Kremlin hospital.

She was on the threshold of a great creative career. In her died a valiant communist who had been directly involved in the liberation struggle and whose lot it had been to write a vivid evocation of it. In her died a communist deeply attached to the Russian working class, but who was also able, thanks to her great culture, to become associated with the revolutionary movement in East and West. In her, lastly, died a profoundly revolutionary woman, a precursor of the new human type which is born in the throes of revolution.

In the words of Lev Nikulin, 'Nature gave her everything: intelligence, talent, and beauty.' She was indeed of an uncommon stamp, and her destiny was far from ordinary. She was a Commissar in the Fifth Army— the army of Ivan Smirnov, Putna and Tukhachevsky, the army that repulsed the Czechoslovaks in their wanderings towards Moscow, which held back Kolchak, shook him badly and retook Siberia. She was a Commissar on the General Staff of the Red Fleet, and a member of the Red Fleet's expedition from Astrakhan to Enzeli. She was the wife of Fyodor Raskolnikov, Vice-President of the Kronstadt Soviet, first Soviet Minister Plenipotentiary to Afghanistan (she left him, however, on their return from that country).

She was sent by the Russian CP's Central Committee to Saxony in 1923, was a belated but enthusiastic witness of the Hamburg insurrection, that unfortunate twist to the failed German Revolution of 1923; and she died of malaria in 1926 at the age of thirty-one.

Even in her death, Larissa Reisner belonged to the realm of legend: for she contracted the disease in Persia, and died of it at about the time when many men, such as Lutovinov, who could not stand the contrast between the days of revolution and civil war and the rule of the Central Committee, where Stalin was still apparently only primus inter pares, were committing suicide. Raskolnikov, a morbidly jealous husband, had treated her roughly, and she became Radek's companion.

Larissa Reisner was, then, a character of some stature. Radek's biography gives her life its true dimension, for it recounts a destiny rather than a mere life. It is significant that Radek, whose style is frequently so verbose, fantastical and humorous, should have given here only a concise outline.

A participant in and witness of many of the decisive events of the Revolution, Larissa Reisner will remain in history as an observer. Radek is right to insist that *On the Front* is one of the best works to come out of the Civil War. These 130 pages are far more effective than volumes of history in evoking the war, from Kazan to Petrograd. That is true to the extent that the selection of works published in the USSR in 1965 contained a very mutilated version of *On the Front*: the original is too close to the truth.

Fyodor Fyodorovich Raskolnikov (1892-1939)

Larissa Reisner's husband Fyodor Raskolnikov, was an active Bolshevik who joined the Russian navy and subsequently became leader of the Kronstadt Soviet. He was a member of the Military Organisation of the Bolshevik Party which planned the October 1917 uprising in St Petersburg and eventually became Commander of the Red Fleet on the Baltic and on the Caspian. His real name was Fyodor Ilyin but like most of his contemporaries in the underground movement, he adopted a pseudonym. In Russian, the word *raskolnik* means dissenter – it was also the name given by Dostoevsky to his murderous protagonist in *Crime and Punishment*. The following passages are extracts from the autobiographical note written by Raskolnikov for the anthology, *Makers of the Russian Revolution:*

I was born on 28 January 1892 in Bolshaya Okhta on the outskirts of St Petersburg. Until 1900 I was brought up by my mother, but in the autumn of that year I was sent to the Prince of Oldenburg's Orphanage, which had the status of a 'modern' school. It was a ghastly institution with the customs of an old-fashioned seminary; pupils were made to kneel in front of the whole class for bad marks, and the chaplain, Lisitsyn, boxed boys' ears in public. I was obliged to spend eight years there as a boarder, leaving in 1908. By this time, I was sixteen. In the seventh form, I had become an atheist, and in the same year became acquainted with the works of Maxim Gorky, Leonid Andreyev and others, which further strengthened my atheism. In 1909 1 entered the Economics Department of the St Petersburg Polytechnical Institute.

At this point, I must briefly describe the formation of my political views. As early as 1905-6, in the fifth and sixth forms, I had twice participated in strikes, and moreover had once been elected to a student delegation which went to see the headmaster with a demand for improvements in living conditions. For this I was nearly expelled. My interest in politics and my sympathy for the revolutionary movement were first aroused by the 1905 Revolution, but as I was then only thirteen, I could understand nothing in the disagreements between separate parties..

I called myself quite simply a socialist. My sympathy for the oppressed and exploited was maintained by reading the works of Sheller-Mikhailov, amongst which the novel *An Omelette Needs Broken Eggs* made a particular impression. In this way my political experiences in 1905 and an acute awareness of social injustice led me instinctively to socialism. This inclination found an all the more ready, heartfelt response, as the material conditions of our family were very difficult.

In 1907 my father died, and mother was left with two sons. Her pension of sixty roubles per month only covered day-to-day expenses, whilst an education had to be found for myself and my younger brother Aleksandr (who now works in the Party under the name of Ilin-Zhenevsky). For lack of resources, the latter had to be transferred from the 'modern' school, where he was a boarder, to the Vvedensky Gymnasium. By running into debt, however, mother managed to let me finish secondary school and also, for a while, to pay for me at the Polytechnical Institute. During subsequent terms, in view of our difficult financial position, the board of professors sometimes exempted me from tuition fees.

During my first year there I had occasion to read Plekhanov's works, which made me a Marxist. In summer 1910, I made a thorough study of *Das Kapital*, and in December of the same year I joined the Party. After publication of the first edition of the legal Bolshevik paper *Zvezda*, I went to its offices, declared my full agreement with the paper's line, and offered my services to the editorial staff. The godfather of my literary work for the Party was K. S. Eremeyev.

From this moment, I became a very close collaborator on *Zvezda* (*The Star*) and *Pravda* (*The Truth*). After beginning with the diary of events, I graduated to articles, the first of which was printed in spring 1911. During this period, I also worked with V. M. Molotov in the Bolshevik group of the Polytechnical Institute and maintained contact on its behalf with the St Petersburg Committee.

When *Pravda* appeared on 22 April 1912, I became editorial secretary. But I only lasted one month in this post since on the night of 21/22 May I was arrested and taken into custody. I was accused under Article 102 of membership of the RSDRP. After solitary confinement lasting four and a half months, I was condemned to three years' exile in Archangel province, but this was replaced by an exit visa. On 9 October I reached Germany, but not far from the border, at Insterburg, where I had stopped to rest for twenty-four hours, I was arrested by the German police and accused of espionage on behalf of Russia. The main evidence was a sketch of the émigré quarters in Paris which Eremeyev had drawn for me before my departure. After a few days I was released and made my way back to Russia with a view to working underground, but at Verzhbolov, on the frontier, I was arrested and deported to Archangel. At Mariampol, however, I fell ill and was confined to bed. By this time, the nervous shock of imprisonment was making itself felt and I was soon given permission for treatment in a sanatorium near St Petersburg.

On 21 February 1913 I benefited as a student from the amnesty and so reacquired the right to reside in St Petersburg. Naturally, I immediately resumed my collaboration on *Pravda*, which for censorship reasons was appearing under various, frequently changed names. With the arrival of L. B. Kamenev from abroad in spring 1914, my participation increased. By then long articles which I wrote to order for the editorial board were appearing as commentaries. I visited *Pravda* almost daily, and from time to time the offices of *Prosveshcheniye* (*The Enlightenment*), which also printed articles of mine. With the outbreak of war, *Pravda* was suppressed. I escaped arrest only by chance since on that day I had finished my work earlier than normal and gone home just before the police arrived.

From the first days of the imperialist war I adopted an internationalist, Leninist position. I helped compose the collective reply to Vandervelde. The war turned me, like other contemporaries, into a military man. Having long been attracted by the elemental life at sea, I joined the navy and despite the lack of a certificate of political reliability, I enrolled for individual classes for naval cadets. During these years I managed to sail on two cruises to the Far East, visiting Japan, Korea and distant Kamchatka. The February Revolution found me sitting my final cadetship examinations.

I immediately made contact with the Petrograd Committee and with the newly reappeared *Pravda*, which had arisen like a phoenix from the ashes. In it I wrote a series of articles until, at the end of March, I was sent by the editors of *Pravda* to Kronstadt to take charge of the local Party organ *Golos Pravdy* (*The Voice of Truth*).

In 'red' Kronstadt I could not limit myself merely to editing the paper, and I threw myself into the thick of Party and Soviet activity. We formed a friendly, tightly knit group which included S. G. Roshal, Kirill (Orlov), P. I. Smirnov and myself, and a little later on were joined by Smilga, Deshevoy, Bregman and Flerovsky.

I was soon elected Vice-Chairman of the Kronstadt Soviet (the Chairman was a non-Party man, Lamanov, who during the subsequent Kronstadt rebellion in 1921 revealed his White Guard views). After the July demonstration, in which I and other people from Kronstadt took an active part, I was arrested, imprisoned in the Kresty and accused of being involved in 'the case of the Bolsheviks'. On 13 October I was released and a few days later was ordered by the Party to Novgorod and Luga to prepared the October Revolution.

During it I was directly involved in the Pulkovo battles. After the defeat of Kerensky's and Krasnov's bands, I was sent as leader of a detachment of sailors to the aid of the revolutionaries in Moscow. I was soon summoned from there and appointed Commissar of the Naval General Staff, then member of the Collegium of the Naval Commissariat and, in 1918, Deputy People's Commissar for Naval Affairs. In June 1918, I carried out a secret mission in Novorossiysk for the Sovnarkom, scuttling the Black Sea Fleet to prevent it from falling into the hands of the imperialist powers. In July 1918 1 was directed to the Czechoslovak Front as a member of the RVS of the Eastern Front, and on 22 August I was appointed Commander of the Volga Naval Flotilla, which actively assisted in the capture of Kazan on 10 September, and then pursued the White Guard flotilla with daily engagements up the Kama river, finally driving them into the Belaya river and obliging them to take refuge in Ufa.

We succeeded in clearing the Kama of White Guard bands beyond Sarapul as far as Galyan. Then ice started forming and our flotilla was forced immediately to make for Nizhny Novgorod to winter there. I returned to Moscow where, as a member of the RVS, I took part in all its sessions and directed the Naval Commissariat together with the late Vasily Mikhailovich Altvater.

In late December 1918 1 set off on a reconnaissance trip to Revel on board the destroyer *Spartak*. We came across a greatly superior British squadron of five light cruisers with six-inch guns. Whilst beating a retreat back to Kronstadt, our vessel suddenly ran aground, smashing the propeller. So, after being captured by the British, I was taken to London and put in Brixton jail. After five months' captivity I was exchanged for nineteen British officers imprisoned in Russia. The exchange took place at Beloostrov on 27 May 1919.

Immediately on my return from England, I was appointed Commander of the Caspian Flotilla. Soon it was joined by the Volga Flotilla, which had returned from the Kama, and the combined river and sea-going forces were called the Volga–Caspian Naval Flotilla.

Our vessels had to operate in separate units over a huge area from Saratov on the Volga to Lagan and Ganyushkin on the Caspian. The most bitterly fought battles were near Tsaritsyn and Chornoye Yaro. In both cases our ships were subjected to almost daily aerial attacks. However, the combined actions of the Red Army and the Red Flotilla saved Astrakhan, which had been encircled by White Guards, holding out only thanks to the one railway line linking it with Saratov. Finally, in 1920, the capture of the Aleksandrov fort and the remnants of the White Guard Ural Cossacks, as well as the expulsion of the British from Enzeli, completed the flotilla's campaign.

During the Civil War I was twice awarded the Order of the Red Banner. In June 1920 I was appointed Commander of the Baltic Fleet. In view of our advance on Warsaw, Kronstadt was put on a state of alert to receive British 'guests'. But to our great disappointment Lloyd George did not send a single British ship into Kronstadt waters.'

Footnote:
In 1937, on tour in Sofia, Raskolnikov noticed that his own memoirs on Kronstadt and Petersburg in 1917 had been included in a list of forbidden books to be burned. He was recalled to Moscow in 1938 but refused to return and instead sought exile in France. From Paris, on 17 August 1939, he wrote Stalin an Open Letter, in which he declared: 'You have destroyed Lenin's party, and on its corpse, you have built a new 'Leninist-Stalinist party' which acts as a cover for your personal power…on the eve of war, you are annihilating the conquests of October. "Father of the people", you have betrayed the Spanish revolutionaries.' This declaration appeared in *Dni* (*The Day*), Kerensky's newspaper. Shortly afterwards, on 12 September 1939, Raskolnikov died in Nice, in suspicious circumstances – after 'falling out of a window'.

In 1963 a book was published in Moscow devoted to the *Heroes of the Civil War*. A long article on Raskolnikov concluded in the following terms: 'Fyodor Fyodorovich remained to the end of his days a true Leninist, a Soviet patriot and a fearless fighter for the Bolshevik Party.' The author of another article on Raskolnikov in *Voprosy Istorii* (*Questions of History*) mentioned the existence of the Open Letter, and wrote that it 'unmasked Stalin's arbitrariness, the discredit which he cast on Soviet democracy and on socialism. Raskolnikov accused Stalin of massive repression of innocent people. He accused Stalin's *Handbook of the History of the CPSU* of robbing those the General Secretary himself had killed and calumnied, and of ascribing their achievements to himself.' Raskolnikov was posthumously rehabilitated in 1963.

✪ FURTHER READING:

Hamburg at the Barricades – and other writings on Weimar Germany, by Larissa Reisner, translated from the Russian and edited by Richard Chappell. Pluto Press 1977.

The Women's Revolution – Russia 1905-1917, by Judy Cox, Haymarket Books 2019

Larissa Reisner, by Cathy Porter, Virago Press 1988.

For the Voice, by Vladimir Mayakovsky and El Lissitsky, 1923, Facsimile dual language edition, The British Library 2000.

Six Red Months in Russia: An Observer's Account of Russia before and during the Proletarian Dictatorship, by Louise Bryant, New York, George H Doran 1918.

Ten Days That Shook the World by John Reed, Penguin Classics (New edition) 2007

My Life: An Attempt at an Autobiography, by Leon Trotsky, Pathfinder Press 1970.

Arthur Ransome in Revolutionary Russia, Two-volume box-set: *The Crisis in Russia* and *Six Weeks in Russia* by Arthur Ransome, Redwords 1992

Year One of the Russian Revolution', by Victor Serge, translated and edited by Peter Sedgwick, with a preface by Paul Foot. Published jointly by Bookmarks and Pluto Press in London, Writers & Readers in New York 1972.

Red Victory: A History of the Russian Civil War, by Bruce Lincoln, Cardinal Non-Fiction 1991.

The White Armies of Russia – A Chronicle of Counter-Revolution and Allied Intervention, by George Stewart, The Naval and Military Press, 2009 .

The Russian Revolution and the Baltic Fleet: War and Politics, February 1917-April 1919, by Evan Mawdsley, Macmillan Press 1978.

The Russian Baltic Fleet in the Time of Ware and Revolution 1914-1918, *The Recollections of Admiral S N Timirev,* Seaforth Publishing, 2020.

Lenin: The Revolution Besieged. 1917-1923, by Tony Cliff, Pluto Press 1978.

Trotsky: The Sword of Revolution 1917-23, by Tony Cliff, Bookmarks 1990

Trotsky: The Prophet Armed 1879-1921, by Isaac Deutscher, Verso Books (New edition) 2003.

The History of the Russian Revolution, by Leon Trotsky, translated by Max Eastman, Penguin Books 2017

Anna Akhmatova: Poet & Prophet, by Roberta Reader, Allison & Busby 1995.

Makers of the Russian Revolution: Biographies of Bolshevik Leaders, by Georges Haupt and Jean-Jacques Marie, translated from the Russian by C.I.P. Ferdinand, *Commentaries* translated from the French by D.M.Bellos, George Allen & Unwin. 1974

Women Journalists in the Russian Revolution and Civil Wars: Case Studies of Ariadna Tyrkova-Williams and Larissa Reisner, 1917-1926, by Katherine

McElvanney, *Revolutionary Russia,* 30:2. 2017.

Sviyazhsk, by Larissa Reisner, translated by John G Wright and Amy Jensen, *Fourth International,* Vol. 4, No. 6. June 1943.

Literature and Revolution, by Leon Trotsky, translated by Rose Strunsky and first published in 1925. Redwords. 1991.

The Russian Experiment in Art, by Camilla Gray, Thames & Hudson. 1986

The Cinema of Eisenstein, by David Bradwell, Harvard University Press 1993.

Eisenstein, Cinema, and History, by James Goodwin, University of Illinois 1993.

Constructivism in Film: The Man with the Movie Camera, A Cinematic Analysis, by Vlada Petric, Cambridge University Press 1993.

Kino-Eye: The writings of Dziga Vertov, translated by Kevin O'Brien, Pluto Press 1984.

Atlas of Russian History, by Martin Gilbert, Dent 1993.

The Raven, by Edgar Allan Poe, with illustrations by Gustav Doré. 1885

ON FILM:

October 1917 – Ten Days That Shook The World, directed by Sergei Eisenstein, Starring Nikolai Popov. First released in 1927 to celebrate the 10th Anniversary of the Bolshevik Revolution. Eureka DVD. 2000.

The Eisenstein Collection – Volume 1: *Strike / Battleship Potemkin / October.* Tartan Video. 2010

Extraordinary footage of the events described by Larissa Reisner appear in the documentary film **Anniversary of the Revolution** made in 1919 by the pioneering Soviet film-maker, Dziga Vertov. This film was recently restored by the Russian film archivist, Nikolai Izvolov, and can be seen on YouTube.

Also available on DVD are:

Man With a Movie Camera, directed with original score by Dziga Vertov, BFI

La Sixième Partie Du Monde + La Onzieme Année directed by Dziga Vertov. 2-DVD Set. In German / Russian / English, with subtitles, music by Michael Nyman.

Kino-Eye & Three Songs About Lenin made by Dziga Vertov, 1934. Russian DVD.

Films made by Dziga Vertov during this period, but not yet freely available, include:

Agit-Train of the Central Committee, directed by Dziga Vertov. Moscow Cine Committee of the People's Commisariat of Education and the All-Russia Central Executive Committee. 1921.

The History of the Civil War, directed by Dziga Vertov. All-Russian Photo-Cine Department (VFKO) and the People's Commissariat of Education. 1921

Cine-Pravda N. 13: Yesterday, Today, Tomorrow, *A Film Poem* dedicated to the October Revolution / October Cine Pravda', author and director Dziga Vertov. Intertitles by Alexander Rodchenko.

Also from Redwords:

Revolution in Danger
by Victor Serge
Translation by Ian Birchall

Brings together three pamphlets never before available in
English - 'During the civil war', 'The endangered city'
and 'The anarchists and the experience of the Russian
revolution'. Written in a Russia under siege these writings
radiate enthusiasm for the achievements of the new society
while remaining alert to the dangers that threatened the
revolution.

ISBN : 9781872208084
£5.99

https://bookmarksbookshop.co.uk